PRAISE FOR

UNDERSTANDIN
THE POWER OF Y~~~~ ~~~~~~~~~

MW00648545

In *Eureka!* Dr. Salisbury has produced the finest integration of hypnosis, self-hypnosis and intuition I have seen. It will become one of the texts in our school and I highly recommend it for all who wish to enhance their intuition.

> —From the foreword by C. NORMAN SHEALY, M.D., PH.D.
> founding President, American Holistic Medical Association,
> author of *Life Beyond 100—Secrets of the Fountain of Youth.*

Readers who have the opportunity to spend some time with Anne, or work with her, have much to gain from one of the most gifted intuitives of our time. This book not only teaches you about intuition but also helps you discover your own intuitive abilities.

> —From the introduction by STANLEY KRIPPNER, PH.D.
> past President, Association for Humanistic Psychology, author of
> *Human Possibilities—Mind Research in the USSR and Eastern Europe.*

If you have ever wondered about intuition, or how you can use it in your career or personal life, this book is for you. It provides a great historical overview of the role intuition has played in the lives of many great thinkers, leaders, innovators and business executives. You quickly realize that having and accessing intuition is a natural gift that we all possess. *Eureka!* provides you with solid ideas, specific tools and exercises to help you get in touch with your intuition.

> —DAN HOFFMAN
> Founder & CEO, Market Perspective,
> Professor of Marketing, Daniels College of Business, University of Denver

Anne Salisbury, Ph.D., deserves praise. She guides the reader through the mystical and the mundane methods of developing intuition. She highlights how some of the most successful business executives have developed and used their intuition. Salisbury provides methods that you can use to enrich your life and open the doors of intuitive perception that are available to all. As a psychologist interested in intuition I wish that I had access to this book years ago.

> —FOWLER C. JONES, ED.D.
> Associate Clinical Professor in Psychiatry, Division of Psychology,
> University of Kansas Medical School

Although in-depth knowledge and a highly focused work ethic are essential for business entrepreneurship, even more important is the ability to make a rapid response to the questions at hand based on intuitive judgment and the ability to reach a conclusion. These are the important ingredients for success in business management. Dr. Anne Salisbury has provided valuable insight into this process.

—JAMES M. KEMPER, JR.
former Chairman of the Board, Commerce Bancshares

Our fast paced global business environment requires that we make decisions without having sufficient time to do the desired data gathering and analysis. This requires executives to develop and trust their intuition for 21st-century success.

Dr. Salisbury's extensive experience and thorough research has produced a practical guide for awakening and developing your innate gift of intuition.

—THOMAS LECRONE
Founder & CEO, LeCrone Management Group

Anne Salisbury has written a compelling, inspiring and very informative book. This is a must read for those interested in helping themselves and others develop a more whole life. This book may be one of the most important publications on intuition to the present date. Anne has made it clear that "the intuitive mind is a sacred gift and the rational mind is a faithful servant."

—JOAN PUTTHOFF, M.A., M.ED.
Founder and President of Joan Putthoff and Associates,
theologian, psychotherapist, educator

Philosophers, theologians, mystics, artists, poets, novelists, scientists, inventors and entrepreneurs have all used intuitive insights to make breakthroughs in their fields. How did they do it? What are the processes involved? Psychologists beginning with Freud, Jung and Assagioli have charted the operation of intuition and the obstacles that prevent it. Anne Salisbury, herself an intuitive as well as a trained psychotherapist with experience in business and the arts, brings a wealth of information and insight to the intuitive process. Her book will help readers develop and apply this universal ability to life's challenges.

—JOSEPH P. SCHULTZ, PH.D.
Distinguished Professor of Judaic Studies, Emeritus;
Director Center for Religious Studies, Emeritus, University of Missouri

The last decade has witnessed an explosive renewal of interest in the role of intuition in decision making. *Eureka!* offers a comprehensive approach to assist managers, indeed any decision maker, in restoring intuitive knowing to its rightful place in personal and professional decision making.

Eureka! pulls together a variety of resources that aid a decision-maker in harnessing the power of intuition. Special attention is given to the processes of self-hypnosis and meditation as decision aids. Based on extensive experience in the field, the author "synthesizes" an integrated process for increasing the flow of intuition. Many authoritative quotes celebrating intuition are sprinkled throughout the text. These inspiring observations of thinkers past and present are a treat in themselves.

Eureka! would have been my choice for a student guide had it been available when I developed and taught courses on "Intuition in Management."

—BILL TAGGART, PH.D.
Professor of Management, College of Business Administration,
Florida International University, *The-Intuitive-Self.org*

Anne Salisbury brilliantly ushers us into the next great frontier of human consciousness—the realm of intuition. Salisbury reveals the great power that lies within us and the incredible transformation that can take place once we tap into and follow the direction of our intuitive thoughts. It is amazing how the genius of so many great figures in history came about as the result of using intuitive powers. Salisbury reveals how you, too, can tap into this great power that lies within.

As a result of her work, I awakened to the intuitive function of consciousness inherent in all humans. I also discovered why I am the way I am and how I can move beyond many of my more fearful reactions to certain situations.

—REV. DUKE TUFTY
Chairman of the Board, Unity World Headquarters

Open any page and get going with your own intuitive development. A scholarly, practical and very readable work—enjoy this tour of the intuitive field from the ancients to modern researchers for gaining insight and inspiration!

—JAMES WANLESS, PH.D.
author of *Intuition@Work, Intuition-Blog.com*

ALSO AVAILABLE BY ANNE SALISBURY

Books, AudioBooks and eBooks
The Intuition Factor (2013)
The Eureka Research: Experiences of Intuition in a Self-Hypnosis Experiment

CDs and DVDs
How to Be More Aware in Relationships (lecture CD)
Introducing Intuition (lecture CD)
Intuitive Meditation (meditation CD)
Your Ideal Body (self-hypnosis CD)
Smoking Cessation: Lecture & Demonstration (DVD)
Weight Management: Lecture & Demonstration (DVD)

Distance Learning Courses
Intuitive Skills I: Tools for Life
Intuitive Skills II: Tools for Inner Sight
Intuitive Skills for Relationships
Intuitive Skills for Creating What You Want
Fundamentals of Hypnosis
Transpersonal Hypnotherapy
Medical Hypnotherapy
Transpersonal NLP (Neuro-linguistic Programming)
Weight Issues

- For books, audiobooks, ebooks and CDs visit *GoIntuition.com*.
- For CDs, DVDs, distance learning courses, and professional certification trainings in hypnotherapy and intuition, visit *TranspersonalInstitute.com*.
- For speeches, seminars, and training for your group or business visit *GoIntuition.com*.
- For business consultations, individual intuitive counseling, energy clearing/feng shui, and pet psychic readings visit *GoIntuition.com*.

Order this book from your local bookseller or by visiting *GoIntuition.com*.

Please visit:
GoIntuition.com (main site)
TranspersonalInstitute.com (distance learning)

EUREKA!

Understanding and Using the Power of Your

INTUITION

Anne Salisbury Ph.D.

Foreword by C. Norman Shealy, M.D., Ph.D.
Introduction by Stanley Krippner, Ph.D.

EUREKA!

UNDERSTANDING AND USING THE POWER OF YOUR INTUITION

by Anne Salisbury, Ph.D.

© 2008, 2013 All rights reserved.

Visit GoIntuition.com

First Edition, published by Morgan James Publishing, was catalogued as follows:

Publisher's Cataloging-in-Publication (Provided by Quality Books, Inc.)

Salisbury, Anne. Eureka! : understanding and using the power of your intuition / Anne Salisbury ; foreword by C. Norman Shealy ; introduction by Stanley Krippner.

p. cm.

Includes bibliographical references and index.

1. Intuition. 2. Self-actualization (Psychology) 3. Decision making—Psychological aspects. 4. Success in business—Psychological aspects. I. Title.

BF315.5.S25 2008   153.4'4

QBI08-600089

ISBN 978-0-9758509-2-3 (paperback)

ISBN 978-0-9758509-3-0 (ePub)

LCCN: 2012920066

Cover by Nick Zelinger, NZGraphics.com

Interior design by Serff Creative Group, Inc., SerffCreative.com

Published in USA by Lively Spirit, Inc.

Second Edition

Books may be purchased for sales promotion

by contacting the publisher,

Lively Spirit, Inc. at P. O. Box 18409, Golden, CO 80402

(800) 375-9703 • 303-474-3071 Fax • info@LivelySpirit.com • LivelySpirit.com

ACKNOWLEDGMENTS

I would very much like to thank two strong proponents of intuition, Norman Shealy and Stanley Krippner, who respectively wrote the Foreword and Introduction to this book. In 1987, I began my hypnotherapy practice at The Shealy Institute for Comprehensive Pain and Health Care. Later, during my doctoral program, I worked with both Norm and Stan to produce the research study that was the inspiration for this book.

I would also like to thank the many authors referenced in this book for putting pen to paper and bringing awareness to this important topic called intuition. In my research I have attempted to understand their many positions, although with any interpretation there is always some guessing around the edges.

My clients and students have brought me joy as I have watched them awaken to their intuitive abilities. Their journeys have motivated me to produce this work.

Also, I would like to express my gratitude to family and friends who see the value in living a life filled with intuition. They helped me in the evolution of this book through their support and feedback. In particular, I am grateful for the sharp-minded input from my mother, Physsie, and my sister, Ellen. And I am thankful for the light-hearted encouragement of my husband, Greg Meyerhoff, with whom I developed *The Eureka System*.[SM]

This book is dedicated to all of you who choose to walk the path with intuition.

CONTENTS
BRIEF VERSION

CONTENTS
LONG VERSION

FOREWORD
By C. Norman Shealy, M.D., Ph.D.

Dr. Shealy is world renowned for his pioneering work in the fields of pain management and alternative forms of treatment. He is a Harvard-trained neurosurgeon, the founding President of the American Holistic Medical Association, President of the International Society for the Study of Subtle Energy and Energy Medicine and the President of Holos University Graduate Seminary. He has written scores of articles and books including the widely acclaimed Life Beyond 100—Secrets of the Fountain of Youth *and* The Creation of Health: Merging Traditional Medicine with Intuitive Diagnosis, *which he co-wrote with Caroline Myss, Ph.D.*

Eureka! What an exciting word with a fascinating history. Undoubtedly human beings have survived for many thousands of years using the inherent power of intuition. All animals and humans also have inborn instincts—unconscious reactions or behaviors that assist in the process of survival. In those individuals who are raised in a nurturing environment, the only natural fears are loud noises and falling. Other fears develop from experience; individuals who are traumatized physically, sexually or emotionally, develop far more instinctual fears than those who are lovingly nurtured. Fear blocks intuition.

Most people consider intuition to be a sixth sense—knowing without experience or training. Actually all great discoveries are the result of intuition—art, music, poetry, scientific discoveries, novels and movies. Many great creative geniuses would be shocked to learn that some people are afraid of intuition. Through the years, especially during the last century, intuition was studied and described under a variety of different terms—psychic phenomena or ability, clairvoyance, extra sensory perception, chance, synchronicity and even magic. A rose by any other name is still a rose. And intuition is one of the great roses of the human mind.

Interestingly, hypnosis and self-hypnosis have also been misunderstood and at times attacked at least as vehemently as intuition. Mesmerism, the forerunner of modern hypnosis, was violently opposed by the Establishment. In the 1840s, Dr. John Elliotson introduced mesmerism into England and demonstrated that the mesmerized individual became clairvoyant, even developing the ability to make medical diagnoses. James Esdaile performed thousands of operations with patients under mesmeric trance. He also wrote a classic book *Natural and Mesmeric Clairvoyance*. It took over 125 more years for hypnosis to be grudgingly and inadequately accepted by physicians and psychologists.

As early as 1912, J. H. Schultz demonstrated that 80% of stress illnesses (and all illnesses are the result of cumulative stress) could be cured with his simple Autogenic Therapy approach. Autogenic Training is one of the most widely studied and successful approaches to self-regulation. Although Schultz did not like to call it what it is, Autogenic Training is a formalized self-hypnotic approach to life. Olympic athletes, students and business people are much more successful when they practice AT regularly. Of greater importance, Schultz reported that individuals who did AT for about six months began to have spontaneous spiritual images and enter meditative states. He actually felt that no one should do meditation until they had balanced themselves with the habit of AT.

In the first half of the twentieth century, Edgar Cayce became the best-known clairvoyant diagnostician. In a deep hypnotic trance he gave almost 15,000 "readings," two-thirds related to medicine and health, with an accuracy which some consider to be about 80%. In the early 1970s I began studying medical intuition and have worked with several talented and highly accurate individuals, including Henry Rucker, Dr. Robert Leichtman and Caroline Myss, the last becoming the best-known medical intuitive in the world. Caroline and I began teaching the principles of Vision, Creativity and Intuition in the mid-80s. Ultimately, that training led to the development of Holos University Graduate Seminary.

In the 70s, Herbert Benson started with a simple form of meditation and determined that regular practice led to improvement in the alarm reaction of stress—namely, that adrenalin and insulin production were lowered by regular practice. He later recognized that he was inducing what he called *The Relaxation Response.*

In *Eureka!* Dr. Salisbury has produced the finest integration of hypnosis, self-hypnosis and intuition that I have seen. It will become one of the texts in our school and I highly recommend it for all who wish to enhance their intuition.

INTRODUCTION
By Stanley Krippner, Ph.D.

Dr. Krippner is recognized internationally for his research on human consciousness, hypnosis, dreamwork, parapsychology and healing. He is a Professor of Psychology and the former President of the Association for Humanistic Psychology and the International Association for the Study of Dreams. Among the numerous books he has authored and coauthored are the renowned Human Possibilities: Mind Research in the USSR and Eastern Europe, Personal Mythology *and* Dreamworking.

I met Anne Salisbury in 1990, when she began her doctoral studies with me. As the strong relationship between her areas of interest and my own work became apparent, Anne asked me to be on her dissertation committee. It was a position I was happy to fill, given that she had chosen for her project a topic close to my heart—intuition.

In 1996, Anne traveled to Russia as a member of the People to People Psychic Arts Delegation. As the delegation's leader, I had the opportunity to observe her interactions with a number of Russian psychics and transpersonal psychotherapists. During our work on her dissertation, I had learned of her exceptional intuitive abilities, upon which her academic interest in the subject was based. Therefore I was not surprised by her professionalism and ability to communicate effectively on both a practical and intuitive level with the Russians. These qualities have helped to make Anne an important international ambassador in the fields of psychic awareness and intuition.

Throughout her life Anne has used the wisdom offered to her in dreams and meditation. She has studied most of the outstanding writers in philosophy and consciousness studies. But what seems to truly set Anne apart is the rare combination of her deeply intuitive nature with a strong practicality and business acumen.

With *Eureka!* Anne presents a consolidated history of intuition that has been missing from the field. It is important to understand that intuition has been discussed throughout the ages, though perhaps using different terminology. Aristotle may have described intuition in another manner, but today people are tapping this same power while referring to it as a "gut instinct" or something that just came to them "out of the blue."

The great strength of this book, I believe, is that in addition to this historical analysis it offers practical tools for accessing intuition that readers can apply to improve their daily lives. By engaging both the analytical and creative parts of their psyches, this book not only teaches readers about intuition but also helps them discover their own intuitive abilities and learn to put these to use to enhance their personal and professional lives.

I am pleased that Anne has made this information available to a general audience through this valuable book. Those readers who have the additional opportunity to spend some time with Anne or work with her have much to gain from one of the most gifted intuitives of our time.

HOW TO USE THIS BOOK

*My understanding of the fundamental laws of the
universe did not come out of my rational mind.*

—Albert Einstein

Intuition—you have this gift and may have experienced it—that
wonderful moment when you just know something without knowing why or how you *know* it. Creative ideas and answers to puzzling
questions pop into your head out of nowhere, spurring moments of
"Eureka!" and "Aha!" You may have referred to these insights by
saying, "It suddenly hit me" or "I had a gut feeling about that."

But what exactly is it? What is so good about it? What keeps you
from being intuitive all of the time? Can you do something to become
more intuitive today?

WHY READ A BOOK ON INTUITION?

The information on intuition spans thousands of years, and now
you have it compiled into a complete book that defines intuition,
gives you the history, further defines it *and* shows you how to use it.
Whether you are a skilled intuitive or just starting to explore this exciting area, you will find answers here.

Eureka! is a resource that satisfies both your left and right brain
by giving you a thorough understanding of intuition as well as many
creative tools that you can use to achieve your goals. It includes the
Eureka! System, a step-by-step process, which you can begin to
implement today. It also shows you how to apply your intuition in the
workplace and in everyday life.

Where Does the Term "Eureka!" Come From?

The term "Eureka!" is attributed to Archimedes in the third century B.C. As the story goes, King Hiero II of Greece suspected his goldsmith of trickery. He wondered whether the crown, which he had commissioned, was made of pure gold or perhaps partially alloyed with silver. He asked his kinsman, Archimedes, a mathematician, to answer this question as there was no known scientific means for making such a determination.

One day, while Archimedes pondered this problem in the public baths, the answer came to him when he watched the water spill over the sides as he displaced it. He was so thrilled with his revelation that he jumped out of the bath, forgetting his clothes, and ran home naked through the streets, shouting "Eureka! Eureka!" (in English, "I found it!") He had received the flash that the varying density of the two metals of equal weight would actually displace differing amounts of water.

Is Intuition Only for a Chosen Few?

Archimedes had experienced an intuitive flash of intuition— that powerful form of knowing that has interested and perplexed humanity throughout the ages. Yet, as fascinated as people have been with intuition, it is only human nature not to believe anything that cannot be seen. Many have refused to believe that intuition exists at all, insisting that these enlightening experiences must be nothing more than odd coincidences or the work of the imagination. They have also held that it must be some kind of an act of genius or a gift belonging to a chosen few. They often look to religion or science, rather than within themselves, for answers. They have trouble believing that these "miraculous" inspirations can be received not only by the holy and the educated but also by the nonreligious and the less educated... that is, by everyone.

What I Have Learned

Years of research have shown me that many people had intuitive experiences as children, which subsequently decreased over the years. These children were confused, as was I, by people's less-than-enthusiastic responses to their insightful revelations. You, too, may have been told to look elsewhere, rather than within, for knowledge and wisdom.

Throughout history children have been advised to listen to their parents, teachers and religious leaders but not to their own inner voice. They have been taught to get their heads out of the clouds and put their minds into books written by "experts" who know better. They have learned to listen to the people around them instead of to their own intuition. It often takes many years of adulthood before they open themselves up again to their intuition. Yet, whenever we stop listening to that sense of knowing for any amount of time, we lose the benefits that come from the deepest wisdom available to mankind.

As a teenager, immersed in the two pursuits of art and poetry, I had experiences that embodied many aspects of what I know today to be the intuitive process. With amazing ease I was able to draw what I saw illustrated in my mind and write what I heard spoken in my head. These experiences formed an early basis for my continuing interest in methods for increasing the access to this faculty of intuition. This book is the culmination of a lifetime of experiences and years of study.

You, Too, Have This Gift

Although it may be hidden beneath the surface for some people, and play a demonstrable part in acts of genius for others, I believe that we are all born with this amazing gift of intuition. The uplifting fact is that our skill for tapping this faculty can be greatly increased. It is dependent only upon our desire and continued practice.

As a business consultant, intuitive, psychotherapist and hypnotherapist, I have had the luxury of delving deeply into my intuitive mind to help others access their own intuition. I have seen amazing shifts in people's lives when they do this. They gain clarity of vision in their personal relationships, their work improves, their self-confidence increases and their lives becomes easier.

Tapping This Ability

Having also had the privilege of pursuing extensive analytical training, I see the value in analysis as well. Ultimately, it takes the marriage of both our intuitive and analytical minds to function successfully in this world.

Both research and experience have shown me that there are many ways to access this ability, including meditation, self-hypnosis and dreamwork. I have used self-hypnosis since college and later opened my clinical practice in hypnotherapy in 1987. In my doctoral studies I conducted research that looked specifically at accessing intuition through self-hypnosis and found that self-hypnosis is, indeed, one of the important ways through which to obtain inner knowing.

You may be surprised to learn what self-hypnosis really is and how simple it is to use. In this book you will discover how to use it along with many other helpful tools for tapping into your intuition.

What You Will Find in This Book

In Part 1 you will explore the many current definitions and synonyms for intuition—arriving at an understanding of the working definition for the term. You will then take a walk through the past to learn how some of the greatest thinkers have defined and used intuition.

In Part 2 you will discover the various ways in which you can receive intuition. You will learn the many characteristics of successful intuiters as well as those factors that can inhibit your intuition. You will also find ways in which intuition can be applied at work and in your everyday life.

Part 3 is where you begin to put into practice the knowledge you've acquired about intuition. In this section you are introduced to the *Eureka! System,* which outlines seven steps to access your intuition. Many stories of real-life experiences illustrate the intuitive process.

Part 4 gives you powerful tools and techniques for accessing your intuition. Among others, these include meditation, self-hypnosis and dreamwork.

INCREASING YOUR *EUREKA!* MOMENTS

My hope is that by looking at intuition in various ways and grasping numerous perspectives on the topic, you will see your own intuitive potential more clearly and experience the real value of tapping the wisdom that lies within. As you read this book and begin to have more of your own *Eureka!* moments, please feel free to e-mail me and let me know about them. To continue to expand and refine your skills, please refer to the suggested additional resources listed at the end of many chapters.

Most exciting, through the increased and consciously accurate use of your intuition, you can make a significant difference in the world. History has proven this to be true for so many individuals. As you look at every aspect of human existence, from science and technology to art and spirituality, you begin to see that intuitive insights are not just for the gifted few—they are for each of us in every day of our lives.

—Anne Salisbury, Ph.D.

PART 1

Intuition Through the Ages

Intuition is more accurate than scientific knowledge.

—Aristotle

"What is intuition?" "Is it real?" "Does everyone have it?" These are some of the most commonly asked questions I hear. So to begin with...

- Chapter 1 – You receive a working definition of intuition and a summary of the material explored in-depth in Chapters 2 through 5—material that was used to arrive at this concluding definition.
- Chapter 2 – You take a walk through history to discover what the ancients had to say about intuition.
- Chapter 3 – You are privy to the thoughts of philosophers, psychologists, scientists and mystics on the subject.
- Chapter 4 – You explore how modern thinkers have contributed to this wealth of knowledge.
- Chapter 5 – You discover the many mystical approaches to intuition.

This investigation through time is designed to satisfy your analytical mind—to give you a full understanding of this mysterious faculty called "intuition." Once you know what intuition is, you can more easily embrace the seeds of wisdom set forth in the following parts of this book.

To give you a look ahead, in Parts 2, 3 and 4 you learn more about intuition, how it works, how you can access it and how you can use the simple *Eureka! System* to apply it in your life.

CHAPTER 1
FIRST THINGS FIRST: DEFINING INTUITION

The intuitive mind is a sacred gift and the rational mind is a faithful servant. We have created a society that honors the servant and has forgotten the gift.

—Albert Einstein

What exactly is intuition? You could say that...

> *Intuition is the act or faculty of knowing immediately, directly and holistically without rational processes and without being aware of how you know. It is also the channel through which you access realms of universal truth, absolute knowledge and ultimate reality.*

This working definition encompasses the many qualities and aspects of intuition that were discovered during my years of research and personal exploration. This synthesizes the wealth of information that is to follow.

COMMON TERMS RELATED TO INTUITION

Throughout history and throughout the world, many words and phrases have been used to describe this faculty that is commonly called intuition today. Some of these terms are used in everyday speech and others are used in particular professions, endeavors, philosophies and spiritual traditions. You may be familiar with many of these:

EVERYDAY TERMS

coincidence
gut feeling
hunch
instinct

intuitive flash
sixth sense
synchronicity

EDUCATIONAL TERMS

educated guess
foresight
genius

giftedness
talent
wisdom

ARTISTIC OR CREATIVE TERMS

breakthrough experience
breakthrough state
creativity
higher creativity

illumination
imagination
insight
poetic imagination

SPIRITUAL OR RELIGIOUS TERMS

absolute knowledge
absolute truth
absolute wisdom
absorption into
   ultimate reality
bliss
channeling
clairaudience
clairsentience
clairvoyance
cosmic consciousness
deep intuition
divination
enlightenment
epiphany
extrasensory perception
higher self

higher state of awareness
illumination
inner light
inner listening
inner voice
inner wisdom
inspiration
kinesthesia
mediumship
mystical state
nirvana
precognition
premonition
prophecy
prajña
revelation

Spiritual or Religious Terms (cont.)

samadhi
satori
self-realization
soul guidance
supreme knowledge
telepathy
transcendence
the absolute Tao

the Good
the Tao
transcendental wisdom
ultimate knowledge
ultimate reality
union with God
universal truth

Colloquial Expressions Describing Intuition

People have attempted to describe their intuitive experiences throughout time. Each age and culture creates its own colloquial expressions to convey that "Eureka!" experience of an intuitive flash. Throughout the world, and in different tongues, similar meanings are conveyed. You may have used some of these common expressions yourself:

a picture came to me
a thought popped
  into my head
aha!
an idea dawned on me
an idea struck me from
  out of the blue
eureka!
I have a feeling
  in my bones
I have a good feeling
  about this
I just have a nose for it
I just know it

I played it by ear
it all suddenly
  became clear
it came from somewhere
  outside of me
it came in a flash
it hit me like a
  lightning bolt
it just feels right
it suddenly hit me
it was a moment of truth
my gut told me
something clicked
  into place

Descriptive Terms

Additional terms to describe this experience have been introduced by the many thinkers discussed later in Part 1 of this book. They refer to intuition as:

- an immediate occurrence
- a non-rational experience
- an open channel
- a path to truth
- an expression of psychic or spiritual forces
- a path to ultimate reality
- a basic psychological function
- a human faculty of mind
- a zone of consciousness in the mental plane
- a way, method or mode of knowing
- a form or basis of knowledge

Common Definitions

Intuition has been described in common dictionaries and encyclopedias as well as dictionaries of epistemology, etymology, philosophy, psychiatry and psychology. In these examples, you can see how the definitions vary even though they are following common threads:

- *Webster's Third New International Dictionary* (unabridged version) states that the term intuit stems from the Latin word intuitus, which translates as "to know or apprehend directly or by intuition." Intuition is defined as, "The act or process of coming to direct knowledge or certainty without reasoning or inferring: immediate cognizance or conviction without rational thought."[1]

- The *World Book Encyclopedia* refers to intuition as, "Knowledge that comes to a person without any conscious remembering or formal reasoning."[2]

- The *Glossary of Epistemology/Philosophy of Science* states that intuitive knowledge is that which "is neither directly based on sense experience nor the product of conscious deductive or inductive inference from premises based on sense experience."[3]

- *A Concise Etymological Dictionary of the English Language* notes that intuition stems from the Latin intueri, which translates as "to look upon."[4]

- *A Dictionary of Philosophy* refers to intuition as, "A form of uninferred or immediate knowledge."[5]

- The *Psychiatric Dictionary* states that intuition is, "A literary and psychological term with no exact scientific definition or connotation. It refers to a special method of perceiving and evaluating objective reality. Intuition differs from foresight, conscious perception and judgment in that it relies heavily on unconscious memory traces of past and forgotten experiences and judgments. In this way, a storehouse of unconscious wisdom that had been accumulated (in unconscious memory) in the past is used in the present."[6]

- *The Dictionary of Psychology* defines it as, "(1) direct or immediate knowledge without consciousness [or awareness] of having engaged in preliminary thinking; (2) a judgment made without preliminary cognition."[7]

- The *Penguin Dictionary of Psychology* defines intuition as, "A mode of understanding or knowing characterized as direct and immediate and occurring without conscious thought or judgment... the process is unmediated and somehow mystical."[8]

IMMEDIACY AND DIRECTNESS

The definition of intuition that we began with includes the qualities of *immediacy* and *directness*. These are similar in that they refer to events that occur without interruption or intervention. *Immediacy* refers to the fact that intuition is not mediated and is received without delay—the apprehension or reception is instantaneous. *Directness* refers to the quality of reception that occurs without diversion.

If an intuition is correct, you can assume that it has been received directly from the intuitive realm. This means that it has not been mediated through the realm of the senses because that could fractionalize the information. You can, however, *interpret* an intuition through the senses, given that you are born with mental, emotional and sensory receptacles.

Many, including the mystics, agree with this assessment. They see no involvement of the senses in receiving intuition because that would mean that the intuition enters through an intervening realm. They see the realm of the senses as separate and less pure.

HOLISTIC RECEPTION

The term *holistic* refers to the idea that you can intuitively receive the total knowledge of a situation, principle or thing as a whole. This is known as the intuitive flash.[9] Because of its holistic nature, it is wise to remain calm and let the information flow in and filter through you in its wholeness, rather than allow fragmentation that would destroy its purity. In other words, when you are receiving intuition, it is important to let the knowledge of what is true come into your awareness without interference or interpretation for the intuition to remain as complete and true as possible.

NON-RATIONAL PROCESS

The one quality that seems to have universal acceptance with all researchers is the non-rational aspect of intuition. The rational or reasoned approach is used to analyze and understand matter. The non-rational mode of intuition is used to know ultimate truth. You know intuitive truths without knowing, rationally, how you know them. You can only know intuitive truths through the intuition.

UNIVERSAL TRUTH

In our definition and throughout history, intuition has been described as universal truth or that which accesses universal truth. The term *truth* can be defined as, "a fundamental or spiritual reality conceived of as being partly or wholly transcendent of perceived actuality and experience."[10] Both intuition and truth are universal in that they exist outside of the material universe and are therefore not limited by it—they transcend everyday reality and experience.

Absolute Knowledge and Wisdom of the Absolute

The terms *knowledge, wisdom* and *understanding* are often used interchangeably by many writers to describe intuition. Delineating these three terms can be challenging because their definitions somewhat overlap. The *Merriam-Webster Dictionary*, for example, defines *knowledge* as, "understanding gained by actual experience," "clear perception of truth" and "something learned and kept in mind." It defines *wisdom* as "knowledge," "insight" and "accumulated learning." *Understanding* is defined as, "knowledge and ability to judge: intelligence." And the ability to understand is defined as the ability to "comprehend" and "interpret."[11] Taken as a group, knowledge and wisdom seem to involve more perception and insight, whereas understanding can involve more comprehension.

You could say that your intellect brings you only general knowledge and rational understanding or comprehension. In contrast, your intuition brings you absolute or ultimate *knowledge* and *wisdom* of the absolute.

Ultimate Reality

It could also be said that intuition accesses ultimate reality as well as the realms of universal truth and absolute knowledge. Sages and those who have attained spiritual mastery experience mystical union with all of these realms. The intuition, not the intellect, knows ultimate reality.

Unconscious, Preconscious and Superconscious Considerations

There are many opinions about the source of intuition. One psychiatrist holds that the intuition is retrievable from the *personal* or *collective unconscious*. Another psychiatrist states that we receive information unconsciously from the senses, while still another holds that intuition is an unconscious realization. One educational researcher hypothesizes that intuition is a *preconscious* process.[12] A psychiatrist, on the other hand, states that the *superconscious* sphere is the seat of intuition.[13] And a mystic holds that the *intuitive mind* resides in the mental plane of the *superconscient*, which is above the *ordinary mind*.[14]

The *unconscious* can be defined in a variety of ways. If the *unconscious* is described as the "absence of participation of the conscious ego," then this seems to be correct because the intuition is accessed without the participation of the ego.[15] And when intuitive knowledge has the feeling of being previously known, then the usage of the word unconscious seems appropriate. However, when the *unconscious* is defined as "psychic material not in the immediate field of awareness," which has been "barred from access to consciousness by some intra-psychic force such as repression,"[16] this characterization does not seem to meet our notion of ultimate truth.

The *preconscious* can be defined as a conglomeration of "thoughts, memories, and similar mental elements that, although not conscious at the moment, can readily be brought into consciousness by an effort of attention."[17] Intuition, however, cannot be "readily brought to consciousness" at will as it is received immediately and spontaneously. Therefore, referring to intuition as a preconscious process does not seem to fit.[18]

The *superconscious*[19] or *superconscient*[20] seems to be the home of intuition. It is more understandable that pure or uncontaminated intuition comes from this realm.

INTUITIVE CHANNELS

How you receive an intuition has been understood or described in many different ways over the years. One thinker asserts that the intuition descends through channels of communication originating at the *superconscious* sphere, the seat of intuition.[21] Another states that intuition flows through an *intuitive process* from your full soul into your higher self—the incarnated portion of your soul—and then into your consciousness or personality. It can also flow through *intuitive channels* from other souls or advanced intelligences into your higher self and then on into your consciousness.[22]

To explain it in a different way: Your questions to the universe flow up intuitive channels, or conduits, to the source of intuition. Intuitive information then returns to you through those same pathways, passing from ultimate reality into your full soul, on into your higher self and finally into your consciousness or personality. Other channels, or information pathways, can originate at the source and flow through the full soul of other intelligences before flowing into your higher self and then on into your personality. These alternate channels bring you different intuitive information because it comes through the perspective of another as opposed to the perspective of your own full soul.

To illustrate this process, you could imagine currents of energy streaming along thin electrical wires originating at the source and connecting into the top of your head. You could also see yourself as possibly having additional wires that originate at the source and flow through other souls or intelligences before connecting into your head. Electrical charges move up and down these conduits like messages moving back and forth across telegraph wires.

In both instances you are accessing ultimate reality through the process of accessing your intuition. Once you have received the intuitive information through the channels available to you, then you translate this pure information through the consciousness of your five senses. If your personality is polluted—for example, by repressed anger—your intuition can be distorted. Depending upon the amount of distortion, the intuitive information that is finally received at the conscious level could be true, and therefore an intuition, or false, and therefore not an intuition. If there is only minimal distortion, it could be that it is simply difficult to decipher the information or correctly interpret that which you have been given.

RECEPTION POINT

The point within you that receives information from the intuitive realm is the "third eye,"[23] or brow chakra, according to Eastern and Western mystics and researchers. The brow, or sixth, chakra is located within the central part of the forehead between the eyebrows and is associated with the pineal and pituitary glands. This is the energy center involved with clairvoyance or "clear vision."[24] It is the seat of intuition.

The chakras are subtle energy centers that cannot be seen by physical eyes. There are at least seven major centers associated with the physical body. The "third eye" is the non-physical one utilized by the intuition. According to Matthew 6:22, "If therefore thine eye be single, thy whole body shall be full of light."[25] In referring to this reception point of intuition, the mystic, Yogananda, notes that,

> *This omniscient eye is variously referred to in scriptures as the third eye, star of the East, inner eye, dove descending from heaven, eye of Shiva, eye of intuition and so on.*[26]

TYPES OF INTUITION

Intuition has been divided by some researchers into two general types to identify the ends of the intuitive spectrum from the more commonplace to the contemplative, awe-inspiring or sublime. The terms they use, however, differ. One, for example, describes these two types as *day-by-day* and *real spiritual* intuition. Others make their delineation between *creative* and *higher* intuition.[27] A similar division can be seen between Western and Eastern views of intuition. In general, Western thought focuses primarily on intuition as a problem-solving tool for everyday life, whereas Eastern thought views intuition more as a path to enlightenment.

REVIEW QUESTIONS

1. What is the one element of intuition that seems to have gained universal acceptance?

2. How is intuition immediate and direct?

3. How do you receive intuition holistically?

CHAPTER 2

INTUITION FROM ANCIENT GREECE THROUGH THE AGE OF REASON

I decided that it was not wisdom that enabled
[poets] to write their poetry, but a kind of instinct
or inspiration, such as you find in seers and prophets
who deliver all their sublime messages without knowing
in the least what they mean.

—Socrates (469-399 B.C.)

The rising interest in intuition appears to be a modern phenomenon. You may be surprised to discover that it has been contemplated for thousands of years. Beginning in the sixth century B.C., we have records of philosophers who were obsessed with the desire to comprehend the meaning and source of truth and knowledge. In the translations of their writings we find the use of the word intuition.

In the earlier part of our walk through history with these Western truth seekers we visit Greece at its height and Rome in its decline. We travel Europe during the Middle Ages, the Renaissance and the Age of Reason. We view twenty-four centuries highlighting the principal philosophers, mathematicians, astrologers and theologians. Their discoveries and opinions are fascinating and revealing.

ANCIENT GREECE

PYTHAGORAS

Pythagoras (582-507 B.C.), the Greek philosopher, astronomer and mathematician felt that fundamental truth could only be explained through numbers because these contained the essence of all things and all relationships. In translating Plato's *Republic* from the original Greek, it was discovered that Pythagoras believed that "numbers themselves, existing in an intuitively apprehended realm, could yield profound knowledge about the universe that was unavailable elsewhere."[1]

PLATO

Plato (427-347 B.C.) in his later writings assigned credit to things not rational as did his teacher, Socrates, who heard an inner voice. Both believed in dreams and the Delphic Oracle as a source of guidance. To them, the irrational soul, through a mysterious "giveness," was the source of intuitive insights for the seer, the poet and those engaged in spiritual pursuits. This type of intuitive information, or "true opinion," was not considered to be part of the intellect and therefore had to be judged, subsequently, by the rational mind.[2]

ARISTOTLE

Aristotle (384-322 B.C.), Plato's student, wrote more fully on the topic of intuition. He held that experience and intuitively known truths were a necessary part of any scientific inquiry. In his *Posterior Analytics (Bk. II; Ch. 19)*, Aristotle stated:

> *Now, of the thinking states by which we grasp truth, some are unfailingly true, others admit of error—opinion, for instance, and calculation, whereas scientific knowing and intuition are always true: further, no other kind of thought except intuition is more accurate than scientific knowledge.*[3]

ARCHIMEDES

Archimedes (287-212 B.C.), the Greek mathematician, physicist and inventor, gave us the first intuitive phrase that we still use today when we have an intuitive experience. He was sitting in the bath when suddenly an intuitive flash came upon him. This solved the problem he had been pondering for days. He jumped up and shouted, "Eureka!" or, in English, "I have found it!" He had intuited the method for determining the purity of gold in the royal crown.[4]

PLUTARCH

In the first century the philosopher Plutarch (46-120 A.D.) stated that, "of the sentences that were written on Apollo's temple at Delphi, the most excellent and most divine seems to have been this: Know thyself."[5] "Know thyself" has become "the central touchstone for psychotherapy ever since."[6] It is considered to be the potion for truth. Just as recipients of ancient Greek oracles were expected to use their intuition to find meaning in those messages, so are modern clients in psychotherapy encouraged to open up to new information given to them through their own intuition.

PLOTINUS

The first significant Greek school of thought that intensely concerned itself with the study of non-rational thought or intuition was that of the Neoplatonists. Plotinus (204-270 A.D.) was the founder of this school and the greatest of the Greek mystics in the late Classical period. In one of his many passages about the "One" being the transcendent origin of all, Plotinus stated:

> *If you grasp it... you will be filled with wonder. And, throwing yourself upon it and coming to rest within it, understand it more and more intimately, knowing it by intuition.*[7]

THE RISE OF ROME

Eventually Rome overpowered Greece and became the dominant influence in the Western world. With the rise of Rome, the emphasis began to shift from an interest in originally inspired art, poetry, drama, architecture and philosophy, which had flourished in Greece (c. 500-100 B.C.), to the more linear areas of administration, law, engineering and architectural design. In the era of the Roman Empire, the educated classes came to embrace more rational disciplines such as stoicism, skepticism and empiricism. They spent less time contemplating the more intuitive arts, so there were fewer works written on intuition during this period. The less educated population, however, continued to support seers and astrologers.

Saint Augustine

Toward the end of the Western Roman Empire, Saint Augustine (354-430 A.D.) appeared. After struggling with numerous philosophies, he converted to Christianity and presented the world with a Christian form of Neoplatonism. He came to believe that the human being's ultimate purpose was to know God. According to Augustine, knowledge resided in the soul and people needed to look within to a non-rational source for their ideas. Inner learning was a "remembering" and a "discovery."[8]

Saint Augustine believed that absolute truth was obtainable from God through the soul. Receiving such truth, or ultimate knowledge, required belief and depended upon the grace of God.[9]

The Middle Ages

From the fall of the Roman Empire in the fifth century to the Renaissance, the Reformation and the discovery of America by Columbus in 1492, Western Europe experienced what is now known as the Middle Ages. Christian inspirations occurred with more frequency during this medieval period. It was during this time that the word intuition or *intuitio* (Latin) was used to describe mystical experiences with God. These revelatory experiences of intuition, however, were reserved for theologians and were considered to be the product of contemplation rather than that of a secular pursuit for knowledge of the world. Therefore, there was little growth in the concept of intuition outside of the church in Western Europe throughout this time.[10]

SAINT BERNARD DE CLAIRVAUX

The medieval theologian Saint Bernard de Clairvaux (1090-1173) held the accepted church view on intuition, which was that it accessed only religious truth and was the end result of contemplation.[11]

MEISTER ECKHART

Nearly two centuries later, the German Dominican and mystic Meister Eckhart (1260-1327) based his views of intuition on the New Testament, ideas of former theologians including Saint Bernard de Clairvaux and beliefs of pagan Neoplatonists. Eckhart, who spent most of his life in France, proposed that, although spiritual intuitive ecstasy was a product of contemplation and union with God, intuition was also an important source of intellectual knowledge. In accepting intuition as a source of such knowledge, Eckhart followed in the footsteps of Plotinus, the best-known Neoplatonist.[12]

WILLIAM OF OCKHAM

William of Ockham (?-1349), an English philosopher, theologian and mystic, was influential in keeping the notion of intuition alive in religious as well as secular circles. To him, intuition provided an awareness of something, not an understanding or judgment. It formed the basis and source of all knowledge.[13] He stated:

> *Nothing can be known naturally in itself unless it is known intuitively.... Intuitive knowledge... is... of such a thing that the intellect immediately judges that the thing exists.[14]... Intuitive knowledge cannot be caused naturally unless the object is present...but it could be caused supernaturally.... There can be by the power of God intuitive knowledge concerning a non-existent object.[15]*

THE RENAISSANCE

The Renaissance, the transitional period between the Middle Ages and modern times in Western Europe, spanned the fourteenth through sixteenth centuries. During this time intuition was scrutinized and challenged by the adjudged superior power of reasoning.[16] For example, respect for wise women had waned in the later Middle Ages; they were subsequently hunted down as witches during the Inquisition. These women risked their lives to offer intuitive healing at the secular level.[17]

The focus was on cultural and intellectual advances instead of on intuition. Science and the mystical were divided into two worlds—the known and all that was unknown—more weight being given to the known. According to what can be learned through written materials, there were no significant new theories on intuition during this period.[18]

NOSTRADAMUS

Nostradamus (1503-1566), the French astrologer and physician, was an exception in his time. He was one of the few successful and respected mystics. His predictions of the future, which were professed to have been received in a trance state, are still being discussed today.[19]

THE AGE OF REASON

The Age of Reason, also called the Age of Enlightenment or the Age of Rationalism, blossomed in the 1600s with Descartes and other philosophers, and lasted through the 1700s. The eighteenth century encompassed the time of the Industrial Revolution when cultures that had been rural and agricultural became more urban. Rationalist philosophers believed, on the whole, that truth could best be reached through the use of reason.

RENÉ DESCARTES

Descartes (1596-1650), the influential French rationalist philosopher and mathematician, was considered to be the father of modern Western philosophy. His approach, the Cartesian method, holds a set of rules that, if followed, will lead to intuitive truth and understanding given the limits of each person's capacity. Oddly enough, this revolutionary approach to mathematics was used as the cornerstone of rationalism in the unfolding Age of Reason, despite the fact that the Cartesian method is based on non-rational thinking.

Descartes felt that there were only two mental operations necessary to arrive at the knowledge of things—intuition and deduction:

*Intuition [comes] not from the senses, nor the... imagination,
[but] is the conception of an... attentive mind. [It is] more
certain than deduction.... The proposition intuited must be
clear and distinct... grasped in its totality at the same time
and not successively. Deduction... appears not to occur all
at the same time, but involves a sort of movement... it infers
one thing from another.*[20]

The role played by God in these processes is explained by
Descartes in a letter he wrote to the Marquis de Newcastle in the
spring of 1648. Descartes wrote:

*Intuitive knowledge is an illumination of the soul, whereby it
beholds in the light of God those things which it pleases Him
to reveal to us by a direct impression of divine clearness in
our understanding.*[21]

BENEDICT DE SPINOZA

In the seventeenth century, there were those who restored intuition to a place alongside reasoning as a way of knowing.[22] Spinoza
(1632-1677), the Dutch philosopher, wrote in *Ethics* that knowledge, or
human ideas, come to us in three modes: *opinion, reason* and *intuitive
knowledge*. He describes them as follows:

*(1) opinion... [is] knowledge from random experience and
imagination:... we recollect things and form certain ideas
of them... (2) reason:... we have common notions and adequate [true] ideas of the properties of things, and (3)... intuitive knowledge... proceeds from an adequate [true] idea of the
formal essence of certain attributes of God to the adequate
[true] knowledge of the... formal essence of things.*[23]

Spinoza went on to observe that, "Our greatest happiness, or
blessedness, consists in the knowledge of God alone."[24]

JEAN-JACQUES ROUSSEAU

In contrast to rationalism extant in his time, Rousseau (1712-1778),
a French political and educational philosopher, was a strong believer
in Romanticism. Romanticism was a movement in the arts that devel-

oped in reaction to rationalism and which continued to gain strength in the fields of technology and science. It was a revolt against the belief in the supremacy of the intellect in favor of the emotional, natural and intimate.[25]

Rousseau, in his revolutionary novel on education, *Emile*, espoused that children's feelings were suppressed in the educational system, thus preventing their reception of natural intuitive experiences. He championed a more individually free and natural lifestyle in which a person's innate nature and intuition could flourish.[26] Owing to these revolutionary views, Rousseau was considered suspect to the point of exile by governmental institutions and the hierarchy of the traditional Catholic and Protestant churches. In this period churches were suspicious of any individual claiming to have an intuitive spiritual experience. Churches devalued these experiences to the level of superstition. Years after his death, however, Rousseau's overall philosophy became an important and integral part of the French Revolution.

IMMANUEL KANT

Kant (1724-1804), the influential German philosopher, held the view that human mental processes consist of information from thoughts (concepts), the senses and intuition. The latter two, he believed, were linked together to create sensible intuition. He held that, when these were also linked with thoughts, understanding was created. In Kant's words:

> *Our intuition can never be other than sensible; that it contains only the mode in which we are affected by objects. The faculty, on the other hand, that enables us to think the object of sensible intuition is the understanding.... Without sensibility no object would be given to us, without understanding no object would be thought. Thoughts without content are empty, intuitions without concepts are blind.... The understanding can intuit nothing, the senses can think nothing. Only through their union can knowledge arise.[27]*

To Kant, intuition was given prior to all thought and was therefore the basis for all knowledge. He considered understanding to be the faculty of knowledge whereas imagination was the faculty that represented an object that was not present.[28]

Review Questions

1. What are some commonalities in thought of these writers on intuition?

2. What was the early Christian thinking about intuition?

3. What examples are there to show that intuition was not wholly embraced in these times?

CHAPTER 3

Nineteenth and Early Twentieth-Century Thinkers

Only intuition gives true psychological understanding both of oneself and of others.

—Roberto Assagioli,
psychoanalyst who developed psychosynthesis

As we move forward through the ages, we discover the writings of later philosophers and psychologists in Europe and America. The scope of their discussions has now enlarged to include the paths through which, and the sources from which, we receive intuition. We find talk about:

- the role played by the will
- mystical states of consciousness
- the creative surge and the experience of beauty
- intuition as a psychological function
- *day-by-day* and *spiritual* intuition

Philosophical Thought

Arthur Schopenhauer

Schopenhauer (1788-1860), a German post-Kantian philosopher, enlarged upon Kant's philosophy concerning intuition. He felt that Kant, who stated that intuition was given through the senses, did not sufficiently define its process or content.

In contrast to Kant, Schopenhauer, who has been described as a metaphysical irrationalist, stated that intuition was called upon through the will to provide answers in the search for meaning and understanding.[1] He stated, "Knowledge in general, rational as well as intuitive, proceeds in the first place from the will itself." He also noted that, "Concepts themselves, in their connection with each other, and not in application to sense-experiences... [are] the province of reason, the understanding [of them] being more intuitive, not discursive."[2]

WILLIAM JAMES

During the latter half of the nineteenth century, strict conformist attitudes of the Victorian era squelched the rise of intuition and free emotional expression. Intuitive experiences and greater freedom of expression were, however, embraced within the realm of the arts. William James (1843-1916), the philosopher and founder of American psychology, boldly acknowledged the existence and importance of mystical states of consciousness. He stated that we can classify an experience as being mystical when it has one of the following qualities or characteristics: "ineffability," "noetic quality," "transiency" and "passivity." In defining the "noetic quality," he described the experience of intuition:

> *Mystical states [exhibiting the noetic quality]... are states of insight into depths of truth unplumbed by the discursive intellect. They are illuminations, revelations, full of significance and importance, all inarticulate though they remain; and as a rule they carry with them a curious sense of authority for aftertime.[3]*

HENRI BERGSON

Bergson (1859-1941), the French philosopher who was admired by William James and those rebelling against convention, opposed the prevailing thought of his day, positivism. Positivism held that there could only be knowledge with observable evidence. This philosophy rejected the earlier metaphysical form of knowledge by insisting only that which could be observed through the senses was meaningful.[4]

In contrast to positivism, Bergson professed that we know matter through our intellect while we know *élan vital*, the creative surge of life that is in and around us, through our intuition. He was a romantic philosopher who professed that, through intuition, we could directly and immediately experience prime reality. We could do this through living a creative life and through the creation of poetry, art, acts of genius, worship and love.[5] Bergson defined intuition as follows:

> *Intuition is mind itself, and, in a certain sense, life itself: the intellect has been cut out of it by a process.... Thus is revealed the unity of the spiritual life. We recognize it only when we place ourselves in intuition in order to go from intuition to the intellect, for from the intellect we shall never pass to intuition.*[6]

Intuition was, to Bergson, a nonintellectual way of attaining absolute knowledge. Bergson agreed with Spinoza that it could not be fully explained with words. And Bergson, Spinoza and Descartes all professed that intuition was operating in human lives even though rational methods could not be used to analyze it.[7]

BENEDETTO CROCE

Croce (1866-1952), an Italian philosopher and aesthetic idealist, began writing at a time when there was renewed interest among the romantic philosophers, such as Bergson, on the subject of intuition. In his book, *Aesthetic*, he described four forms of activity: *aesthetic* or *intuitive, logical* or *conceptual, economic* and *ethical.* The first two are both forms of knowledge while the latter two encompass practical activity. According to Croce's philosophy, pure intuition is the foundation for knowledge, and it has no logical components. Logical knowledge, in contrast, can only be formed upon the content and spiritual activity of the intuition.[8]

To Croce, intuition could be described as an image that is formed in the mind. In discussing language, poetry and art, he notes that all of our verbalized or written words and our artistic works are preceded by an internal image or expression:[9] "The feeling and movement which we find in art is something that belongs intrinsically to the intuitive activity—it is the dynamic of the creative process itself."[10]

CLASSICAL VIEWS

The writings of Croce, along with those of Bergson and Spinoza, comprise the three most prominent classical views on intuition. These views allow for no component of reason in the process.[11] They also hold that intuition is "the path to ultimate reality." More specifically, for Spinoza, the intuitive experience is one of knowing God. For Croce, it is to "experience beauty." For both it is direct contact with ultimate reality. And for Bergson, "prime reality is neither God nor beauty, but the experience of pure duration."[12]

PSYCHOLOGICAL THOUGHT

SIGMUND FREUD

Freud (1856-1939), the Austrian psychiatrist who is best known as the founder of psychoanalysis, did not address the subject of intuition.[13] It was Freud's belief that the unconscious was the receptacle of early negative influences, which were the cause of later neuroses and psychoses in the individual.

CARL GUSTAV JUNG

Following Freud in the early twentieth century, greater attention and respect was given to the field of intuition. Jung (1875-1961), the Swiss psychiatrist and founder of analytical psychology, was the first of the early psychologists to deal with intuition in great depth.[14] To Jung, intuition was a "basic psychological function." He stated:

> *My psychological experience has shown time and again that certain contents issue from a psyche that is more complete than consciousness. They often contain a superior analysis of insight or knowledge that consciousness has not been able to produce. We have a suitable word for such occurrences—intuition.[15]*

Jung's theory of intuition was embedded in his theory of personality in which he defined the four mental functions of *thinking, feeling, sensing* and *intuiting.* These were combined with his two attitudes of extroversion and introversion.[16]

Thinking involves judgments of true and false, logical deductions and inferences. *Feelings* involve judgments of like and dislike. Both of these functions are rational, but they cannot operate at the same time.[17]

Sensing involves receiving sensory perceptions and details. *Intuiting* involves receiving, immediately and holistically, perceptions of principles, objects (including symbols) and possibilities. Sensation and intuition are non-rational and non-judgmental. They are both "given," whereas facts are perceived as true. These two functions cannot operate coincidentally.[18] Sense data can be received consciously from either the internal or external world, whereas intuited data can only be received internally. For Jung, intuitive knowledge of empirical truths is nonsensory.[19]

In addition, Jung postulated that the psyche has three levels: the *conscious*, the *personal unconscious* and the *collective unconscious*. The *conscious* mind is readily available to awareness: it contains those thoughts, feelings and perceptions of which we are momentarily aware. It is within the *personal unconscious* that repressed, subliminally perceived and forgotten feelings, thoughts and intuitions reside. The *collective unconscious*, by comparison, is the repository of repressed experiences that are not personal but are, instead, of the society or race. This is the realm of the archetypes, or primordial images, which are passed down from generation to generation as a common heritage. Examples of these are the Wise Old Man and the Earth Mother.[20]

According to Jung, intuitive material is retrievable from both the personal and the collective unconscious. His theory of the unconscious can be explained in this way:

> *Intuitions of the collective unconscious are held by Jung to be generally far more important than are the intuitions of the personal unconscious. The contents of the latter are the undesirable, maladaptive, subliminally perceived, and undeveloped residue of an individual's personal history, while the contents of the former are powerful, fundamental knowings, truths, and systems of symbolism repeated and developed over generations as basic wisdom about recurrent problems of mankind.... The intuitive perceives the potentials, possibilities and implications of these truths and may be able to translate them into the terms of contemporary life.[21]*

Jung felt that, although intuitive facts are accepted as valid, they can be in error, given the storing of incorrect wisdom in both the *personal* and *collective unconscious.*[22] And, because some collectively held beliefs are in error, it can be difficult for members of a culture to accept opposing truths.[23]

Roberto Assagioli

Assagioli (1888-1975), a colleague of Sigmund Freud, Carl Jung and Abraham Maslow, developed *psychosynthesis*—a psychology that sees people naturally tending towards harmony.[24] Assagioli considered intuition to be a means for apprehending reality immediately, directly and holistically rather than in parts and progressively, which is the method by which the analytical mind perceives. He recognized that intuition was being repressed in individuals and society through its devaluation and neglect. He saw that preference was being given to the prevailing analytical mind.[25]

For Assagioli, there were two types of intuition: *day-by-day* and *real spiritual* intuition.[26] *Day-by-day* intuition was afforded the common form of hunches. *Real spiritual* intuition was considered to be the high form of inner vision that could comprehend the essence of reality.[27] Assagioli wrote:

> *Intuition as described by Bergson is predominantly on the personal levels, while intuition according to Plotinus is purely spiritual. Intuition according to Jung is on both of these two levels; and... we will take the Jungian attitude and speak of intuition fundamentally as a function which can be active on different levels, and can therefore assume different aspects but remain fundamentally the same.*[28]

Assagioli proposed that intuition was one of the seven psychological functions that occur either spontaneously or as directed by the will. These are *sensation, emotion-feeling, impulse-desire, imagination, thought, intuition* and *will.*[29] Intuition, according to Assagioli, may be directed by the will albeit in an indirect manner:

> *It seems evident that the will possesses no direct power over the intuitive function; it can even hamper its functioning. But here also the will can perform a most helpful indirect action;*

it can create and keep clear the channel of communication along which the intuitive impressions descend. It does this by imposing a temporary check on the distracting activities of the other psychological functions. The will can encourage... the intuitive operation by formulating questions to be addressed to the superconscious sphere, the seat of the intuition. These questions must be given a clear and precise form. The replies may come promptly but more often they appear after a lapse of time and when least expected.[30]

This important role that Assagioli assigns to the will is reminiscent of Schopenhauer's writings on the subject a century earlier.

ERIC BERNE

Berne (1910-1970), the American military psychiatrist and psychoanalyst who developed the theory of transactional analysis, defined intuition as "knowledge based on experience and acquired through sensory contact with the subject without the "intuiter" being able to formulate to himself or others exactly how he came to his conclusions."[31] Berne differed from Jung in that he believed that intuitive knowledge could be unconsciously received through the senses. Jung believed that only the conscious mind could receive information this way.

GENERAL THOUGHT

ALBERT EINSTEIN

Einstein (1879-1955), the great mathematical physicist, stated, "My understanding of the fundamental laws of the universe did not come out of my rational mind."[32] He noted that he thought almost entirely in images. For him understanding came from the intuitive process of freely playing with images, words and explanations.[33]

BUCKMINSTER FULLER

Fuller (1895-1983), the American philosopher and engineer, took a broad view of the role of intuition by stating that any progress that has been made in history was through the utilization of "intuitive awareness... that eternally reliable generalized principle for all humanity."[34] Fuller stated that intuition allows us to purposefully affect our physical environment. He held that by using our intuition we could move humanity toward physical and metaphysical success.[35]

Review Questions

1. What role do Schopenhauer and Assagioli say the will has in accessing intuition?

2. According to Bergson, is it possible to use your creativity to access intuition, thereby enabling you to experience prime reality?

3. According to Jung, where does intuitive material reside?

4. What are Assagioli's thoughts on intuition?

CHAPTER 4
RECENT FINDINGS ON INTUITION

*We spent [almost none] of our time studying
plans for the mission and [almost all of our time]
learning how to react intuitively to all the "what ifs."
Reliance on the intuitive response was the
most important part of an astronaut's training.*

**—Edgar Mitchell, Apollo astronaut and
founder of the Institute for Noetic Sciences**

Beyond the well-known philosophers and psychologists of the twentieth century, a number of other recent thinkers have made important contributions to the field of intuition. These authors have combined the definitions of their predecessors with their own to develop innovative ideas. Their discussions include:

• the sources of knowledge

• ways to verify an intuition

• the characteristics of intuition

• creativity, insight and imagination

PERCEIVING INTUITION THROUGH A DISCIPLINE

In *Intuition: The New Frontier of Management*, Parikh, Neubauer, and Lank note that intuition continues to be defined through the perspectives of the various disciplines. *Philosophy* looks to the insights of knowledge; *epistemology* considers intuition as a process or skill; *psychology* divides it into traits and attitudes; the *arts* sees it as the source of creative expression; *neuroscience* analyzes its biochemical processes; and *mysticism* explores it as a way of knowing that leads to revealed truth.

Intuition: A Noun, a Verb, an Adjective

Interestingly, Parikh et al. also note that intuition can be referred to as a *noun, verb* or *adjective.* For example, philosophers are concerned with the source of knowledge and truth. So, for them, intuition appears in the form of a noun. Epistemologists research the way in which we intuit what we know and, therefore, use it in the form of a verb. Psychologists analyze individuals to determine if they are intuitive, thereby using it as an adjective. In this way, "An intuitive (adjective) person can intuit (verb) and experience an intuition (noun)."[1]

Without the Aid of Reason

In the early twentieth century the philosopher, K. W. Wild, thoroughly studied the field of intuition and reported the results in her book, *Intuition.* She offered many different descriptions of intuition, and the one definition that was generally accepted by other authors is that, "Intuition is the essential mental act involved in any knowing."[2] Wild eventually came to the conclusion that intuition is a method by which a subject becomes aware, or the immediate awareness itself, "of an entity without such aid from the senses or from reason as would account for such awareness."[3]

Franz Winkler, medical doctor and author of *The Bridge Between Two Worlds*, states that inner sight is a valuable gift that must be reawakened through conscious efforts. To him, "truth, religion, and freedom cannot be perceived by our physical senses: they are real only to immediate experience, to an inner vision... called intuitive perception."[4]

Intuition: A Source of Knowledge

Pitirim Sorokin, an early twentieth-century sociologist, proposed in *The Crisis of Our Age* that there are three sources of knowledge: *intuitive, sensory* and *rational.* Each shows us one aspect of reality: intuition shows us the aspect that is beyond the scope of the senses and logic; the senses show us the non-rational aspect; and reason shows us the rational or logical aspect. Sorokin explains:

*Each source of knowledge—the senses, reason and intu-
ition—affords a genuine cognition of the manifold reality.
Intuition in its ordinary form as a momentary and direct
grasp of a certain reality—the grasp distinct from sensory
perception or logical reasoning—yields a knowledge of this
aspect of reality like, for instance, the certain validity of anyone of us that "I exist."…. Both [reason and the senses] are
ultimately rooted in intuition as a basic postulate of science.[5]*

According to Sorokin, intuition is the spark behind any creative
process. It brings us solutions. It is at the root of scientific discoveries,
the beautiful, moral norms and religious values.

Intuitive, or ideational, truth is revealed supersensorily by God
through mystic experiences and divine intuition or inspiration. This
is what Sorokin identifies as the truth that comes through faith and
gives us absolute, spiritual, nonmaterial knowledge. Sensate truth
comes through the sense organs. And rational, or idealistic, truth is the
synthesis of the previous two. These three truths serve to check each
other so that we can stay on course rather than veering in any one
direction as has unfortunately happened during many periods in history. Sorokin suggests that oscillation between the three can keep our
cultures in balance and bring us integral truth.

REASON USES INTUITION, INTUITION USES REASON

A. C. Ewing, in his lecture titled, "Reason and Intuition," de-
lineated the relationship between the two functions of intuition and
reason: "Intuition becomes a basic process that provides elemental
truths that are used by reason to arrive at inferences and deductions."[6]
Therefore, reason and intuition are dependent upon each other for
arriving at truths. "Reasoning becomes nothing but a chain of intuitions," according to Ewing.[7]

One can begin with reason and use intuition for verification or
one can begin with an intuition and then use reason to establish its
validity. We may use reason to define an intuition even though it may
seem unnecessary.[8] Ewing does believe, however, that there are certain "primitive laws" that are immediately apprehended and accepted
through the intuition without the use of reason. These are accepted as

innately true.[9] This involvement with reason differs from the thinking of K. W. Wild.

Objective, Subjective and Organic Intuition

The philosopher Archie J. Bahm, in his book, *Types of Intuition*, defines intuition as the "immediacy or directness of apprehension.... [One] grasps directly what he apprehends, without requiring inference regarding what is beyond our belief in casual meditation."[10]

Bahm's three types of intuition are defined as follows: *objective intuition* may be defined as "immediate apprehension of external objects."[11] *Subjective intuition* occurs when either "the 'subject' or intuiter may be intuited." And, finally, *organic intuition* occurs "when both object and subject, intuited and intuiter, appear immediately together in apprehension."[12]

Bahm addresses the persistent and popular question concerning the possibility of error in intuitive knowledge. He believes that it cannot be absolutely reliable. "Yet... there is nothing apart from intuition to trust, for whatever we appeal to must be intuited."[13] Bahm holds that intuitive information should be accepted as received unless there is a reason to question it. At that juncture, the only recourse would be to seek further intuitive truths.

Intuition Fills the Gap

Jerome Bruner in his book, *The Process of Education*, and Malcolm Westcott in his book, *Toward a Contemporary Psychology of Intuition*, both assert that intuition can be the instrument that assists us in transcending the current evidence in front of us to arrive at possibly correct judgments.[14] They both believe in the inferential approach.[15]

Bruner defines intuition as, "the intellectual technique of arriving at plausible but tentative formulations without going through the analytic steps by which such formulations would be found to be valid, or invalid, conclusions."[16] According to Westcott, intuition involves, "reaching conclusions on the basis of little information, which are normally reached on the basis of significantly more information."[17] According to both Bruner and Westcott, intuiters are either unaware of, or unclear about, how they actually reach their intuitive conclusions.[18]

INTUITION VS. LOGIC

Tony Bastick, author of *Intuition: How We Think and Act*, stresses the way in which intuition differs from logic. He notes that intuition involves emotions and physical responses; is immediate, instinctive, empathic, preconscious and holistic; and is not arrived at in a linear manner. Logic, by contrast, is emotionless, absent of physical responses, slower, mediated, conscious, fractional and linear.

Bastick is one of the writers who feels the word intuition is synonymous with the word insight. He proposes the following twenty properties or characteristics of intuition or insight:

> *(1) quick, immediate, sudden appearance; (2) emotional involvement; (3) preconscious process; (4) contrast with abstract reasoning, logic, or analytic thought; (5) influenced by experience; (6) understanding by feeling-emotive not tactile; (7) associations with creativity; (8) associations with egocentricity; (9) intuition need not be correct; (10) subjective certainty of correctness; (11) recentering; (12) empathy, kinesthetic or other; (13) innate, instinctive knowledge or ability; (14) preverbal concept; (15) global knowledge; (16) incomplete knowledge; (17) hypnogogic reverie; (18) sense of relations; (19) dependence on environment; (20) transfer and transposition.[19]*

To clarify some of these characteristics, "emotional involvement" is used as it relates to being non-rational. "Influenced by experience" refers to learning from previous experience that may no longer be conscious. "Understanding by feeling" may be interpreted as a sensed or felt insight. "Recentering" refers to an emphasis on concentration and empathy. "Sense of relations" and "transposition" refer to insight into, and an awareness of, relationships. The term "preverbal" includes non-verbal communication in this context. According to Bastick, intuitive knowledge cannot be verbalized or stored verbally.[20] He concurs with Eric Berne and quotes him as believing that, "perception for intuition is preverbal body language communication."[21]

CREATIVITY AND INTUITION

Bastick also explores "associations with creativity" more deeply. Many people are unclear as to the differences between creativity and intuition and often use the terms interchangeably, just as they do insight and intuition. [22]

According to Webster's definition, to be creative is, "to bring something new into existence by inventing it."[23] Sorokin believed that intuition provided the impetus for creativity.[24] To Bastick, intuition is required as the first stage of creativity. According to Jacquelyn Wonder and Jeffrey Blake, who researched and wrote on the subject of creativity:

> *The creative thought process cannot take place without [the] use of both logic and intuition.... Anyone can use logic to look at the process, to look for faulty data, or for new data. At the same time anyone can use intuition to know when to stop looking for more facts, when to allow the mind to form a new pattern, to re-combine the facts. In this way anyone can use logic—as well as intuition—to facilitate the zap or flash of creativity.*[25]

THE ROLE OF THE WILL

Nel Noddings and Paul Shore, in their book, *Awakening the Inner Eye: Intuition in Education*, emphasize the importance of the will in the intuitive process. They assert that the will is the driving force at the core of our being. "Intuition is that function that contacts objects directly in phenomena. This direct contact yields... 'knowledge,'... guides our actions and is precipitated by our own quest for meaning."[26] The intuition's quest for meaning is motivated by the will. Here we see agreement with Schopenhauer and Assagioli as to the essential function of the will.

To Noddings and Shore, reasoning must be strengthened by intuition; otherwise, it is incomplete. Therefore, intuition is used to organize concepts and precepts. "Reason must be looked upon by intuition in order to be seen and understood."[27]

INSIGHT AND INTUITION

In her book, *Artwork of the Mind: An Interdisciplinary Description of Insight and the Search for It in Student Writing*, Mary Murray defines insight as:

> *a type of understanding that results when a person resolves a meaningful dissonance (lack of harmony, which can be either conscious or unconscious) through integrating experiences, attitudes or emotions with the intellect in such a way that the particular resolution is a simple, permanently true, powerful personal knowledge that is used to interpret other dissonances past and future.*[28]

Murray's description of dissonance aligns itself with the prerequisites for intuition: questions, problems to be solved or a hunger for truth. She also notes that insights come effortlessly in a surprising flash, are verified over time and bring us understanding.[29] Previous authors have referred to this process as the process of intuition.

Bastick acknowledges the confusion between the terms "insight" and "intuition" and calls the literature a "semantic jungle."[30] According to Webster's: "To have an insight is to apprehend a situation or oneself and gain immediate understanding. It is the act of seeing intuitively."[31] If there is a difference between the terms "insight" and "intuition," it is debatable.

INTUITION AS A WARNING SIGNAL

In his book, *The Gift of Fear*, Gavin de Becker writes that intuition, as a warning signal, is dependable in two ways: it responds to a stimulus, and the information provided serves our best interest. "Intuition is just listening.... You may have greater confidence in conscious predictions... but that doesn't... increase their accuracy."[32] In contrast to reasoning, he notes, everything the intuition communicates is meaningful and timely. Our interpretation of it, however, is open to possible error.

INTUITION AND IMAGINATION

Frances Vaughan, a transpersonal psychologist, defines intuition in her book, *Awakening Intuition*, as a psychological way of knowing. She distinguishes intuition from imagination by saying that:

> *Pure intuition is knowledge that comes out of the experience of formlessness and silence, whereas imagination gives form to the formless and is conceptual in nature.... Thus, imagination is the vehicle whereby intuition finds expression in life.... Intuition makes use of imagination, dreams, fantasies and other forms of imagery to enter conscious awareness, yet it remains distinctly independent of all these forms.*[33]

To clarify Vaughan's definition a bit further: when you receive an intuition, it is pure truth. You then translate it through the imagery of your imagination to arrive at a meaning that feels right to your intuitive mind and makes sense to your analytical mind. This can happen in an instant without your conscious awareness. Because you have to make sense of formless emanations through imagery, you may sometimes translate the information incorrectly. Therefore you must stay quiet for a time and listen, checking in with your intuitive mind to make sure you have translated the incoming information correctly. You translate intuition using imagery, which can include seeing, hearing, feeling, tasting and smelling.

For example, if you are driving down a road and have the feeling that you don't want to turn at your designated exit, what is that feeling? It is important to take a brief moment and listen to your feelings once again. It could be only your imagination talking. Were you imagining something fearful based on your past? Or was this your intuition showing you images to let you know that there was a problem ahead? It is important to go beyond your imagination to the pure truth of your intuition.

THE ROLE OF INTUITION

Original thinkers in many fields acknowledge the role played by intuition in their ideas and discoveries. Arthur Koestler, journalist, author and nominee for the Nobel Prize, comments on original thinkers:

> *Their virtually unanimous emphasis on spontaneous intuitions, unconscious guidance, and sudden leaps of imagination, which they are at a loss to explain, suggests that the role of strictly rational thought-processes in scientific discovery has been vastly over-estimated since the Age of Enlightenment.*[34]

THE IMPORTANCE OF INTUITION IS RECOGNIZED

In the latter half of the twentieth century there was an upswelling of interest in the field of intuition. In the 1970s, after he experienced profound altered states during his return trip from the moon, Edgar Mitchell, the Apollo 14 astronaut, founded the Institute of Noetic Sciences to research human consciousness.[35] Mitchell felt that the solution to our current worldly problems would come through the development of our intuitive powers.[36]

Weston Agor, while working as the director of the Public Administration Program at the University of Texas at El Paso, also recognized the importance of intuition.[37] In the 1980s he set up the Intuition Network, made up of scientists, mathematicians, psychologists and business people interested in the accessing of intuition.[38]

REVIEW QUESTIONS

1. According to Sorokin, what are the three sources of knowledge?
2. How do reason and intuition rely upon each other?
3. According to Bahm, what should you do if you don't trust your initial intuition?
4. When have you or another experienced intuition as a warning signal?
5. What is the difference between intuition and imagination?

CHAPTER 5

MODERN MYSTICAL APPROACHES TO INTUITION

*The power of intuitive understanding will protect
you from harm until the end of your days.*

**—Lao-Tsu, founder of Taoism,
author of *Tao Te Ching***

Twentieth-century mystics, or those who experience direct communion or mystical union with ultimate reality, have also defined intuition in a variety of ways. Yet there is no evolutionary pattern in their discussions of intuition. Instead, each mystic builds his or her own case independently.

EASTERN AND WESTERN VIEWS

Since the time of the Roman Empire, Western thought developed, for the most part, along the lines of deductive reasoning rather than intuition. Judeo-Christian religions gave us models for our cultures based on law, linear structure, deductive analysis, individualism and future-oriented goals. In the areas of industry and technology, intuition has rarely been valued or encouraged as a tool.

There have been, however, Western mystics and scholars who have nourished intuition, but these individuals have not been in the forefront of accepted thought. In general, Western cultures have supported creativity in individuals mainly in the hopes of advancing social goals.[1]

While Western thought has been struggling with its understanding, definition and acceptance of intuition, Eastern thought has embraced intuition more openly for centuries.

In Eastern philosophy intuition is considered a faculty of mind that develops in the course of spiritual growth... the Buddha taught that intuition, not reason, is the source of ultimate truth and wisdom. In Zen meditation, the discriminating conscious mind is quieted, and the intuitive mind is liberated.[2]

Today, in both the East and West mystics agree that only intuition can grasp ultimate truth.[3] They also generally agree that ordinary intuitive insights and spiritual illuminations are assumed to be received immediately rather than indirectly through the external senses.

According to Vaughan, a Western psychotherapist with Buddhist training, at the spiritual level of awareness, as opposed to the mental, emotional or physical levels, there is no duality and therefore there are no images. This ultimate reality is purely experiential. It cannot be proven through rational means and can only be known through intuition.[4]

Intuition leads always into the unknown, into the experience of reality beyond words, beyond seeing, and beyond knowing.... [It] allows you to see out of the inner prison you build for yourself, and only then can you make conscious choices about what you want to do.[5]

SRI AUROBINDO

Sri Aurobindo (1879-1950), the Asian guru written about in many books, holds that there are four zones of consciousness in the mental plane of the *superconscient* above the *ordinary mind*. These are, "in ascending order, the *higher mind*, the *illumined mind*, the *intuitive mind*, and the *overmind*."[6]

To outline these briefly, the *ordinary mind* sees things linearly and in opposites. The experiences of joy and pain here are lessened by the swirling and jumping of thoughts. The *higher mind*, often found in thinkers, is somewhat clearer and freer, yet it has to explain its experiences to itself in order to understand them.

The *illumined mind* is accessed as the higher mind becomes more silent. This plane is flooded with diffused translucent light and vibrates with an enthusiastic state of awakening to truths that require no understanding. From this luminous state of joy, you are open to channeling the rhythms of art and poetry.

Next, with more equilibrium and silence, there is a move to the *intuitive mind* that sees in isolated flashes and is transparent rather than translucent. Here, knowledge is immediately available and recognized as that which is already known and simply re-experienced through the flash. This is self-discovery. Language in this plane is concise, and this can be seen in the writings of Plotinus and the Hindu mystical scriptures, the *Upanishads*. This intuitive mind language differs from the richer language of the *illumined mind* evidenced in the writings of Shakespeare and Wordsworth.

Sri Aurobindo states that, "The Intuition... sees things by flashes, point by point, not as a whole," and then the mind, "makes at once too little and too much of it."[7] In other words, in grasping to understand the flash, it is diluted and fragmented. Therefore, Sri Aurobindo suggests that:

> *If we could remain quiet during that vibrating flash, as if suspended in its light, without pouncing on it to cut it into intellectual pieces, we would notice after a while that our whole being has changed altitude, and that we possess a new kind of vision instead of a lifeless little phrase. Explaining causes most of the transforming power to vanish.*[8]

Sri Aurobindo suggests that we "Remain quiet during that vibrating flash, as if suspended in its light... Explaining causes most of the transforming power to vanish."

If, instead of trying to explain the flash, we remain in a meditative silence with the desire to be more intuitive, the intuitive flashes will then increase with more regularity and become more whole. We can then move to the *overmind*. This is an experience of, "cosmic consciousness, but with no loss of the individual." In this state of consciousness "large extensions of space and time" are seen in a single glance under a stable, uniform light.[9] This is the birthplace of the poetic, artistic and intellectual revelations as well as inspirations for great religions. Contradictions melt into unity and, "opposites are no longer felt as negations or shadowy gaps between two flashes of consciousness, but as elements of a certain intensity within a continuous cosmic harmony."[10]

Paramahansa Yogananda

Yogananda (1893-1952), in his book, *Autobiography of a Yogi*, notes that, "Intuition is a soul guidance, appearing naturally in man during those instants when his mind is calm." He states that:

All thoughts vibrate eternally in the cosmos. By deep concentration a master is able to detect the thoughts of any man, living or dead. Thoughts are universally and not individually rooted: a truth cannot be created, but only perceived. Any erroneous thought of man is a result of an imperfection, large or small, in his discernment.[11]

According to Yogananda, truth may be accessed through intuition. But when the mind is not calm, guidance or intuition cannot be perceived clearly. It sometimes appears that an intuition is faulty when, in fact, the guidance was imperfectly perceived.

Ram Das and Paul Gorman recommend that we let go of the nagging thinking mind and listen, without grasping, to the quiet mind.

Ram Das

Das and Gorman state in their book, *How Can I Help? Stories and Reflections on Service*, that our intuition surprises us with solutions to problems when we, "function from this place of spacious awareness... free of the prejudices of mind that come from identifying with cherished attitudes and opinions."[12] Whereas we arrive at analytical solutions linearly, we come to intuitive solutions in an instant when we surrender, trust and pay attention to that voice, image or sense within.

To receive answers intuitively, Das and Gorman agree with Sri Aurobindo and suggest that we let go of judging and analyzing. They recommend that we release the nagging thinking mind and listen, without grasping, to the quiet mind. It is only then that we can hear the truth of what is needed.

> *When we have been used to knowing where we stand at every moment [then] the experience of resting in awareness without any specific thoughts to hold onto and trusting our intuition turns out to be a refreshing and exciting adventure. In this choiceless spacious awareness, we don't necessarily know from moment to moment how everything is going to come out. Nor do we have a clear idea of what is expected of us. Our stance is just one of listening... of fine tuning... trusting that all will become apparent at the proper time.[13]*

SWAMI RAMA

Swami Rama, Rudolph Ballentine, and Swami Ajaya in their book, *Yoga and Psychotherapy*, note that intuition is well defined in Eastern psychology. They hold that an intuition differs greatly from that which is commonly termed a "hunch" in the West. A hunch may be defined as a contaminated intuition because there are elements of the personal unconscious that are intermingled with it and cloud its truth. Therefore, a hunch is unreliable even though it is a glimpse into the capacity of the quieted mind. And when the analytical mind realizes its potential and attempts to control the intuition, or a "successful" hunch, the intuition evaporates.[14] In contrast to hunches:

> *True intuition is a stable, reliable function of the higher levels of consciousness and awareness from which a wider range of information is accessible. There intellect and emotion flow together and become integrated, permitting a new kind of knowing, a kind of knowing that both depends on and promotes self-realization. Intuition unquestionably comes from the highest source of knowledge. It grows bit by bit with the growth of consciousness.[15]*

Furthermore, "True intuition may be divided into creative intuition, which involves creating in the physical world, and higher intuition, which is used for introspection into the very nature of our being."[16]

GARY ZUKAV

In his book, *The Seat of the Soul*, Zukav states that most people see themselves as *five-sensory* humans. They think that impulses and intuitions originate within their psyches and are unpredictable. They often act upon "false" intuitions since they rarely understand how these differ from those that are authentic. They also do not know that the information from an authentic intuition can be trusted.

To move beyond this limited perception, five-sensory humans must first be aware that unseen wise and compassionate guidance is continuously available to them through their intuition. Secondly, they must consciously choose to draw upon that assistance.[17]

Gary Zukav holds that wise and compassionate guidance is continuously available to us, and we must consciously choose to draw upon that assistance.

As a *multisensory* human you are continuously aware that you are in communication with your higher self. You have conscious access to the additional sensory system of your intuition, which operates outside of the five senses. Through your intuition you access not only creative ideas and inspirations but also truth, which empowers and "can do no harm."[18]

"From the multisensory point of view... insights, intuitions, hunches and inspirations are messages"[19] from your full soul, the souls of others and advanced intelligences. These messages travel from your full soul through your higher self (the incarnated portion of your soul) into your personality. Zukav titles the transference of intuitive information from your own soul as the *intuitive process* and that from other souls as coming through *intuitive channels*.

ASSOCIATION FOR RESEARCH AND ENLIGHTENMENT

The Association for Research and Enlightenment (A.R.E.), which was founded upon the works of visionary Edgar Cayce, refers to intuition as a way of receiving "answers from within." Once the answers are accessed, they may be brought into consciousness and intuited. A.R.E. and Cayce state that:

We should view [intuition] as quite a natural occurrence—
"the innate expressions of the inner self" (Edgar Cayce,
Reading 276-6).... [It] can be thought of as an expression of
the psychic or spiritual forces while one remains in a con-
scious state.... Dreams and visions are the... most direct way
to experience psychic ability in the unconscious state.[20]

THE THIRD EYE

The so-called "third eye" in Eastern traditions is the seat of intuitive knowledge. According to Ramakrishna, the Hindu mystic, it is
through this opening that we receive "direct knowledge of the supreme
Self."[21] This "third eye," which is located between the two eyebrows, is
the purported brow, or sixth, chakra within the chakra system.

The chakras, or subtle energy centers, take in subtle energy, or
information, and transform it so that it can be utilized in the physical
body. There are at least seven major chakras associated with the physical body. These chakras have corresponding points within the nervous
and endocrine systems.

The chakra system has been discussed extensively by Eastern
thinkers and has also been researched by Western scientists. According to Richard Gerber, medical doctor and researcher,

Anatomically, each major chakra is associated with a major
nerve plexus and a major endocrine gland.... Physically, the
brow chakra is associated with the pineal gland, the pitu-
itary gland, and the spinal cord, as well as the eyes, ears,
nose and sinuses.[22]

Further, the chakras function as subtle organs of psychic perception. "The third-eye center is actively involved in clairvoyant
perception.From the French vocabulary, clairvoyance literally
means, 'clear seeing.'"[23]

In the seventeenth century, the French philosopher René
Descartes drew pictures showing light emanating from this area
on the forehead.[24] He felt that the soul, which is nonphysical, has its
principal seat in the pineal gland, and it radiates from there throughout
the body.[25]

Edgar Cayce, the "sleeping prophet," stated that intuition:

rises along the pineal center to the base of the brain....
It rises then to the hidden eye in the center of the brain system,
or is felt in the forefront of the head... or the bridge of
the nose.[26]

C. W. Leadbeater, in his book, *The Chakras*, states that the sixth chakra is connected to the pituitary gland. Arousing the sixth chakra fully is said to bring about clairvoyance. He feels that the pineal gland, located in the center of the brain, is associated with the seventh chakra, said to be the seat of wisdom.

Jack Schwartz, both a researcher and researchee at the Menninger Foundation, agrees with Leadbeater and believes that the sixth chakra is indeed connected to the pituitary gland while the seventh relates to the pineal.[27]

Caroline Myss, medical intuitive, and Norman Shealy, medical doctor, in their book, *The Science of Medical Intuition*, state that the sixth chakra corresponds in the endocrine system to the brain, which encases the pituitary, pineal and hypothalamus glands. In the nervous system the sixth chakra corresponds to the brain as well. They hold that "the brain is truly the seat of intellect, wisdom, and the integration of intuition."[28]

Author and researcher Zoa Rockenstein considers intuition to be a major function of the brain. She states that intuition is "an open channel to universal sources of knowledge and wisdom that transcends the boundaries of time, space, the senses, and the logical/rational mind."[29]

In the twentieth century a team of neuroscientists studied people who had lesions in their brains in the area of this purported "third eye." These researchers hypothesized that intuition and emotion play significant roles in problem solving. They found that the lesions had not affected the subjects' intellectual abilities or factual memories. However, they had caused the subjects to lose their emotional memories and the ability to experience "hunches" or even indulge in a willingness to hazard guesses.[30]

REVIEW QUESTIONS

1. In what areas does Western culture support or not support the use of intuition?

2. On what point do the mystics of both the East and West agree?

3. What is meant by Zukav's term *multisensory* human?

4. How would you describe the third eye?

PART 2

How Intuition Works

Intuition will tell the thinking mind where to look next.

**—Jonas Salk, microbiologist who
developed the first polio vaccine**

Many people ask, "How do you access intuition?" What makes someone really intuitive?" "When would you want to use it?"

Now that you have a solid working definition of intuition and an understanding of the history behind it, you can next see how it works and what it has to offer you. Specifically...

- Chapter 6 – You discover the many ways you can access and receive intuition.

- Chapter 7 – You read about the various traits of successful intuitors. You may already possess some of these and want to acquire other traits as well.

- Chapter 8 – You find out how you can apply intuition in your workplace.

- Chapter 9 – You learn about potential inhibitors and how you can avoid them.

- Chapter 10 – You come to know the various ideas about the process of intuition. These gave rise to the *Eureka! System*, an easy-to-follow method for accessing intuition, which is covered in Parts 3 and 4.

CHAPTER 6
THE WAYS YOU RECEIVE INTUITION

People have to go beyond the idea of intuition
as a once-in-a-lifetime lightning bolt and beyond
the idea that it is the province of the gifted few or
of oddballs. We all have intuition within us and we
need to take the responsibility to accept, develop
and perfect our own style of it.

—Michael Ray, professor emeritus
Stanford University School of Business

Now it is time to discuss intuition in more realistic and practical terms. You have learned that intuition is immediate, direct and holistic and that it accesses universal truth, absolute knowledge and ultimate reality. But once you experience this pure intuitive flash, how do you receive and interpret it through your physical sensing system?

As you will soon see, you can receive intuition through a variety of modes: physical, emotional, mental, spiritual and environmental. You can receive it through a physical sensation, an emotional feeling, a mental experience of words popping into your head (verbally), a mental experience of images crossing your mind (visually), a sense of knowing and a cue from the environment around you. Information can come to you through symbols and dreams as well.

STYLES OF RECEPTION

Intuitive consultant Nancy Rosanoff, in her book, *Intuition Workout*, refers to three principal "styles" or modes of reception. You will probably experience one dominant style, although from time to time you will have intuitive experiences through the other modes as well. These styles are:

- *kinesthetic* (physical sensations)
- *emotional* (feelings)
- *mental* (images or symbolic images)

Kinesthetic intuitives physically feel knowledge through their bodies. They may have a gut feeling or a pain in their neck—and mean it quite literally. They receive intuitive knowledge via both physical sensations and emotional feelings.

An *emotional* intuition may come in either a vague or specific feeling such as mild depression or elation. Emotional knowledge can be experienced through visual images, physical sensations and emotional feelings.

A *mental* intuition might be experienced as thought in the form of an unexpected or persistent hunch. Usually mental intuitives experience knowledge through visual images and physical sensations.[1]

LEVELS OF AWARENESS

Francis Vaughan, author of *Awakening Intuition*, mentions "levels of awareness," which are similar to Rosanoff's styles of intuitive reception. Weston Agor in his book, *The Logic of Intuitive Decision Making*, gives credit to Vaughan's four levels of awareness or reception in his discussion of the intuitive process.[2] These are the *physical, emotional, mental* and her additional *spiritual level.*

Your intuitive experiences on the *physical level* may go unacknowledged or be interpreted as purely physical problems. Some people, while interpreting physical events as purely the symptoms of bodily problems, act on unacknowledged intuitive information without knowing they are doing so. For example, you could have a stomachache that keeps you from going to work. The stomachache is real, but your intuition could be telling you to stay off the freeway that morning because there is going to be a big accident there.

It is important to become more consciously aware of your intuitive information. As Vaughan explains, "Learning to trust your bodily responses is part of learning to trust your intuition.... The body is one's access to the world."[3]

Your intuitive experiences at the *emotional level* can be received through the visual cues you receive from watching another person. This includes body language, facial expressions and voice tones. You can also gain a holistic awareness of someone with whom you come into contact.

In our rational Western culture, *mental level* intuitive awareness is particularly appreciated. Intuitive experiences at this level often pertain to creative problem solving, science, technology and the areas of mental inquiry. Successful business people typically access mental intuition and literally "see the big picture," utilizing the holistic element of intuition.

At the *spiritual level* of intuitive reception you can receive mystical knowledge and enlightenment. This level does not use external cues from the senses, emotions or thoughts to validate your intuitions. Instead, your intuition comes to you as a sense of knowing—you do not receive physical sensations, emotional feelings or mental images at this level.[4]

Marcia Emery, in her *Intuition Workbook*, proposes a fifth level of intuitive awareness, which she calls *environmental*. At this level, signals from the external environment bring you intuitive information. For example, if your computer goes down just before you print out your last-minute project, this could be a message to you to either stop procrastinating or delay the project all together.[5]

LANGUAGES OF INTUITION

Milton Fisher, in his book, *Intuition: How to Use It in Your Life*, identifies three "languages of intuition," which are the signals or indications that you are receiving an intuition. These languages are *feelings, symbols* and *dreams*. He identifies the feeling you receive from an intuition as distinct from a feeling brought about through rational means. For example, if you have a vague feeling of discomfort and can find no rational source, then it could be that it is an intuitive warning. Yet not all *feelings* are intuitive, and neither are all *symbols* or *dreams*. To determine if they are offering you intuitive information, you must search for the meaning in your own life.

Philip Goldberg, author of *The Intuitive Edge*, describes four "languages of intuition" that correspond in many ways to those styles and levels we have already discussed. These are *physical, emotional, verbal* and *visual*. Intuitive information may appear to the intuiter in only one language or in a combination.

Some expressions for describing *physical* intuitions are, "a glow, a burning sensation, a cold chill, tingling, or electricity running through"[6] you. These sensations can be interpreted as either positive or as warning signals.

The *emotional* language of feelings differs from the physical language of feelings. One emotional reaction could be a positive or negative sense about someone or something. For example, you could know intuitively that someone is lying to you because you feel uncomfortable in his or her presence. You could also feel happy about seeing another acquaintance because you intuitively know that he or she has your best interest at heart.

An example of a *verbal* flash is a word popping into your head that triggers a solution to a question or problem.[7]

A well documented *visual* flash was received by the German chemist, Friedrich August von Kekule. He dozed off in front of his fire and visualized a snake seizing hold of its own tail.[8] This experience provided him with the long-sought after solution for the structure of certain organic compounds.[9]

Beyond the *physical, emotional, verbal* and *visual* "languages of intuition," Goldberg identifies *exceptional* or profound intuitions as those that encompass the emotions of happiness and harmony. *Exceptional* intuitions are in response to greater questions, such as the meaning of life, and these serve humanity through the scope of deeper wisdom. *Exceptional* intuitions are distinct from those that he refers to as *mediocre*. *Mediocre* intuitions occur in response to the more mundane needs of everyday life.

Great minds in the arts and sciences have attested to exceptional qualities of beauty, harmony, balance, symmetry and joy held within intuitive truths. Johannes Kepler, the astronomer, wrote the following response to a dispute about his theory on astronomy: "I have attested to it as true in my deepest soul and I contemplate its beauty with incredible and ravishing delight."[10] With this same conviction, English poet John Keats wrote in his "Ode on a Grecian Urn:"

> "'Beauty is truth, truth beauty,'—that is all Ye know on earth, and all ye need to know.'"[11]

REVIEW QUESTIONS

1. What are the five modes of reception for intuition (often called styles or levels)?

2. What is an example of each of these five modes of reception?

3. What is an example of an *exceptional* intuition?

4. What is an example of a *mediocre* intuition?

CHAPTER 7
CHARACTERISTICS OF SUCCESSFUL INTUITERS

All great men are gifted with intuition.
They know, without reasoning or analysis,
what they need to know.

—Alexis Carrell, Nobel Prize-winning
surgeon/biologist

While it is true that intuition is more developed in some people than it is in others, accessing intuition is possible for everyone. By reading the following stories of highly developed intuiters and learning about their characteristics, you can notice corresponding characteristics in yourself.

JUNG'S INTUITIVE PERSONALITY TYPE

According to the research done using the Meyers-Briggs Type Indicator, a personality assessment tool based on Jung's theory of personality types, people who are more intuitive are also generally more open to changes in their lives. These people tend to be open to future possibilities, enjoy problem solving and are interested in people and situations. They like order in all areas of their lives yet tolerate change. They are apt to grasp an overview of a concept, see the situation as a whole rather than in individualized parts[1] and continually keep the overall problem in mind. They evidence a willingness both to take risks[2] and to make mistakes in seeking solutions.[3]

Robert Hanson, a Jungian psychologist, stated that the intuitive person, "tends to perceive things in terms of possibilities, meanings and relationships. The intuiter has an active imagination, is continually coming up with new ideas, is often inspired, and enjoys tackling new and unresolved problems."[4]

Daniel Cappon, in his article, "The Anatomy of Intuition," differs from those who think in terms of Carl Jung's personality types. He does, however, recognize that there can be elements or traits of a personality that would characterize an intuitive person. For example, he believes that openness, as opposed to rigidity, is an intuitive trait.[5]

Intuitive Skills and Qualities

Cappon divided the skills that characterize an intuitive person into two general groups using computer terminology. In the first group there are ten skills that he assigns to a lower level of passive perception—these are titled *input skills*. In the second group there are nine skills that must be activated by an external event—these are titled *output skills*.

Input Skills

- knowing something after minimal exposure
- identifying something without complete information
- identifying something obscure
- distinguishing objects from one another
- distinguishing items not seen
- seeing the parts and recognizing the whole picture
- recognizing time segments
- seeing the whole picture and remembering the parts
- receiving images spontaneously
- knowing instinctual responses

Output Skills

- creating images
- knowing future events
- knowing the correct time to act
- having a hunch
- choosing the best method to use
- choosing the best application for a discovery
- knowing why or having hindsight
- having the ability to separate unrelated elements
- knowing the meaning of symbols[6]

Malcolm Westcott conducted research on individuals who, "display extreme degrees of intuitive thinking" to determine the qualities they posess.[7] According to his findings, highly successful intuitive thinkers are:

- resistant to external traditional order and social controls
- somewhat uncomfortable in leadership positions
- nonconforming and comfortable about being so
- confident
- self-sufficient
- willing to manipulate situations for a purpose
- highly self-controlled
- involved in abstract issues, primarily intellectual and ethical
- comfortable with uncertainty and ambiguity
- open to criticism, accepting or rejecting it as appropriate
- willing to accept challenges
- willing to change when necessary
- independent
- spontaneous
- self-determined
- comfortable with suspending judgment and taking risks
- lacking rigid demands for verifiability or justification
- moral while questioning others and ignoring societal pressures
- suppressed in affect except within their own pursuits
- not interested in identifying with groups
- possessed with high goals and aspirations[8]

Successful intuiters are apt to keep a problem that is under consideration constantly in mind, although not always at the forefront. They have a belief in the intuitive process and a willingness to participate in the process, which has a positive effect on the clarity and frequency of their intuitions.[9] In fact, the stronger their motivation for a successful outcome and the larger their store of knowledge on a particular subject, the greater their intuitive leap. These intuitive leaps may be referred to "acts of genius."[10]

Intuitive thinkers are more flexible and spontaneous than systematic thinkers. The systematic thinker breaks down the problem into smaller pieces, analyzes it in an orderly yet time-consuming fashion and then makes a plan for action. Intuitive thinkers, on the other hand, take the broad view, imagine possible alternatives, move quickly between ideas, deal with many problems at once and use hunches. This saves time, but the intuitive thinker may miss some aspect that the systematic thinker might have located through the more laborious approach.[11]

There is a popular notion that many geniuses and exceptional artists are disorganized. This is not an accurate description of many intuitive thinkers. For example, one account of Immanuel Kant, the highly intuitive philosopher, states:

> *He lived a mechanically ordered and abstract old bachelor life... rising, coffee drinking, writing, reading college lectures, eating, walking, all had their fixed time, and neighbors knew that it was exactly half past three when Immanuel Kant in his grey coat, with his bamboo cane in his hand left his house door and went to Lime Tree Avenue.*[12]

Bill Kautz, founder of the Center for Applied Intuition, asserts that the only two traits that all intuitives have in common are the, "willingness to develop their intuitive abilities and... a more spiritual outlook on life."[13] Kautz also identifies some further traits that many intuitives have that appear to foster intuitive insights: an interest in music or other nonverbal arts, entrepreneurial talents, an expertise in diagnosis, honesty and clarity in communication, comfort with being alone, good listening ability and emotional sensitivity.[14]

PERSONAL POWER

The medical intuitive Caroline Myss, in her book, *Anatomy of the Spirit*, is firmly convinced that we need to have faith in ourselves and trust our insights to be more intuitive. Successful intuitive work cannot be possible if we lack a sense of personal power, confidence and self-esteem. To develop these qualities, as well as attain spiritual maturity, we must go through four stages: *revolution, involution, narcissism* and *evolution.*

In the first stage, *revolution*, we separate from our tribe or social group and learn to stand on our own, relying on our individual inner guidance. In the second phase, internal *involution*, we concentrate on ourselves in an attempt to gain inner strength so that we can cope with life. In the third stage, *narcissism*, we spend time in "indulgence of the self."[15] This is generally accompanied by external criticism from the tribe. In the last stage, *evolution*, we once again go inside to develop a firm sense of inner confidence and self-esteem that is powerful enough to withstand life in the external world. It is from this position of strength that we can successfully receive intuitive information.

Myss agrees with Vaughan that our attention should be focused in the present moment to receive intuition.[16] We need to be free of fear and take risks in opening up to and acting upon the information we receive.[17] And to ensure that the information we receive is pure rather than contaminated, there needs to be no emotion involved either in the search for, or the analysis of, the insight. According to Myss:

> *Intuitive ability is present in everyone because it is a survival skill, not a spiritual intention. Maintaining a reflective or meditative attitude, however, facilitates your reception of intuitions. Objectivity will help you interpret the impressions you receive and put them into a symbolic spiritual context.... Clear intuition requires the ability to respect your own impressions.[18]*

CHILDREN, WOMEN, MEN AND THE HOME ENVIRONMENT

Many researchers in the field note that children typically display more intuitive traits than do adults. And because adult males are usually more associated with rationality and hold the more dominant position in Western culture, both women and children are considered to be the opposite and thus more intuitive.[19]

Because women have been in the traditional care-taking role for so long, they have, as a group, developed greater sensitivity to intuition within human relationships than have most men. As caretakers they have had to sense intuitively the needs of their children. In addition, in the past women have been denied education and have therefore had to rely on means other than trained logic to function in our society.[20] These facts may have resulted in increased intuitive experiences for women. However, if the gender roles imposed by society were to be removed, it is assumed that these differences would disappear. It is also assumed that there is no variance in the innate intuitive capabilities of men and women.[21]

Men who are functioning in more traditional male roles may find, sometimes to their disappointment, that they are much more intuitive in the workplace than they are in their personal relationships. This is because their material survival depends upon their success at work, making them more motivated to become intuitive in this arena. They may also be less motivated to become intuitive in relationships because they do not see them as survival situations. If, however, they were to switch their primary focus to the home, or if they were to equalize their focus on both work and home, then it could be assumed that they would become intuitive in personal relationships as well. Likewise, women who have been functioning in more traditional homemaking roles may also become more intuitive in the work environment as that becomes more of a survival need or an area of their expertise.

In an interesting study involving participants raised in "low nurturant" homes, the researchers concluded that these individuals had developed above-average intuitive abilities. The assumption was that this development resulted from the subjects' need to rely on their own inner sense of knowing which, in turn, brought forth their intuitive skills. These individuals had to put aside their intellectual capacities and depend, instead, more heavily upon their own intuition.[22] Childhood dependence on intuition, as a coping mechanism in response to the stress of growing up in "low nurturant" homes, lasted into their adulthood.

In other individuals, however, the stress that arises in adulthood generally calls forth different coping mechanisms, which block the ability to access intuition. Stress can thus have a negative impact on intuitive abilities in most adults.

CREATIVITY

As you have seen in the historical overview, the relationship between intuition and creativity has long been pondered. Many now believe that intuitive guidance is the foundation[23] for divergent thinking in creativity.[24] Creativity, which is often a product of intuition followed by logic, actualizes our human potential[25] by bringing something new into existence.[26]

Some individuals are creative in many aspects of their lives whereas others are creative in only one particular area. Some may excel creatively in an avocation, perhaps owing to the natural lack of external controls, whereas others may excel vocationally.[27] As Mihaly Csikszentmihalyi explains in *The Evolving Self:*

> *Every human being has this creative urge [stemming from intuition] as his or her birthright. It can be squelched and corrupted but it cannot be completely extinguished.[28]*

Intuitive individuals have a moderate to high level of pre-occupation with innovative ideas. They also have a sense of commitment to their involvement with these ideas.[29] Highly intuitive and creative individuals can become obsessed with innovative activities.[30] According to Philip Goldberg:

> *Intuiters... are stimulated by abstract ideas and by implications and relationships among concepts; they like doing things their own way; the unknown, the complex and the novel attract them.[31]*

EXPERTISE AND BUSINESS SUCCESS

There is yet another group of intuitive individuals—people who are experts in their own field. Through their experience and expertise they have not only accumulated, but also internally organized, vast amounts of information. This heightened awareness has increased their instances of intuitive thought because they are able to relax into their area of expertise. However, this power of increased intuition may not necessarily extend to areas beyond their field.[32]

Weston Agor, university professor and management consultant, found that the business arena is a natural laboratory for measuring successes and failures in using intuition. He outlined several personality traits of intuitive individuals that he believes are identifiable in business:

- a positive self-image
- independence in setting goals and reaching decisions
- an ability to come up with new ideas when external data are lacking
- an assumption of risks
- maintenance of a focus on the solution.[33]

As you will see in the next chapter, many managers, successful entrepreneurs, company presidents and CEOs exhibit common personality traits. Their success in business can be linked to their intuitive skills.

Review Questions

1. What are several qualities of highly successful intuitive thinkers?

2. How can you develop your personal power to enhance your intuition?

3. How do traditional gender roles potentially affect intuition?

4. In what area of your life do you feel you have some expertise? How do you experience yourself as being more intuitive there?

CHAPTER 8
THE POWER OF INTUITION IN THE WORKPLACE

You have to ask a lot of questions and listen to people, but eventually, you have to go by your own instincts.
—Kirk Kerkorian, billionaire investor

When your intuitive skills are applied in the workplace, the results can be significant. You can achieve a sharper focus, become more creative in problem solving, make more reliable decisions and ultimately make more money for yourself and your company. It is called by many names, yet it is still intuition.

In the business environment intuition is quantifiable through sales figures, income statements and other means. Therefore, research has been conducted to identify it and determine which methods can be used to increase this skill. Given the positive findings, more business schools and companies are beginning to promote its use.

THE ESCALATING IMPORTANCE OF INTUITION IN BUSINESS

A hallmark of the late twentieth and early twenty-first century has been an explosion of information and our ability to access it. At this point in history you can read, watch and listen to material on nearly any subject and at any time. Using intuition has become almost essential in decision making precisely because of this plethora of data. Management guru and business author Tom Peters notes that:

> *Intuition is the new physics. It's an Einsteinian, seven-sense, practical way to make tough decisions. The crazier the times are, the more important it is for leaders to develop and trust their intuition.*[1]

And Microsoft's Bill Gates, who has played an enormous role in creating this unprecedented access to information, has himself stated quite succinctly, "Often you have to rely on your intuition."[2]

Of course the use of intuition in business decision making is not new. If you recall that intuition can most simply be described as, "knowing without being aware of how we know," then you can probably think of occurrences in your own life that demonstrate the way in which intuition has played a key and successful role in many of your important decisions. Remember times when you had a "gut feeling" or "instinct," or explained a decision or a sudden knowing by saying, "I just knew it," "It suddenly hit me," "Something clicked into place," "The solution suddenly became clear," or "It just felt right."

A number of business and intuition researchers point out that perhaps because of our evolving self-view as a rational, technologically driven society, we are generally more comfortable accepting the role of intuition in our personal lives than we are in our professional settings. Nancy Rosanoff, for example, who has consulted with numerous national and international companies on the topic of intuition, tells of a two-year study of senior managers conducted by Daniel Isenberg and reported in the *Harvard Business Review*. According to Rosanoff:

> *[Isenberg] found that although the majority of managers favored the intuitive over more analytic approaches, most believed it was not how decisions were normally handled by other successful managers. This... statement tells us that intuition is used, but seen as "wrong" or "not normal" by the managers who use it. Managers use intuition and feel isolated in their practice.[3]*

Yet highly successful managers and business executives—perhaps the more seasoned, or those not in fear of losing their jobs—generally acknowledge that relying on intuition is an essential part of their decision making process. Stanford Business School professor emeritus, Michael Ray, cites research indicating that, "it is often impossible for managers to use rational forms of decision making since the situations in which they operate are so chaotic."[4] Ray also points out that this use of intuition by successful managers is not merely a matter of being a necessary fallback approach to chaotic situations but, in fact, indicates a positive correlation between intuitive ability and managerial success:

> *There have been personality inventories and various tests used to measure individual intuition, and scores on them correlate positively and significantly with managerial ranking (higher ranked managers scored higher on the intuition tests) and ability (profit performance of the company or division managed).*[5]

The only mistake I ever made was not listening to my gut.
—Lee Iacocca, former chairman of Chrysler
and world-renowned industrialist

PERSONALITY TRAITS OF SUCCESSFUL INTUITIVE BUSINESS PEOPLE

During the past two decades, many psychologists and business researchers have studied this connection between intuitive ability and professional success to identify personality traits of accomplished intuitive business people. As discussed in the previous chapter, Weston Agor, who views the business world as an ideal setting for the study of intuition's role in success, outlined five key personality traits of intuitive business people:

- positive self-image
- ability to set goals/reach decisions independently
- ability to generate new ideas without external data
- willingness to take risks
- ability to maintain a steady focus on the solution.[6]

Jagdish Parikh, Fred Neubauer, and Alden Lank also outlined several intuitive traits that they found to be important for business success. Drawing on the Meyers-Briggs Type Indicator, they used groups of traits to define four types of intuitive managers. The first in the list, the *troubleshooters*, are independent, impersonal and initiate projects. They are spontaneous, have the ability to see the big picture, welcome change and use non-rational reasoning to gain a feel or solution for a situation. Next are the *facilitators*, who work more closely and effectively with people, understand and inspire them. Third are the *creators*, who are imaginative innovators and reorganizers. Last are the *harmonizers*, who typically thrive on problems and are good at solving them while centering mainly on the welfare of those around them.[7]

Author Roy Rowan interviewed a number of highly successful business people to put his finger on the personality traits of what he termed *intuitive managers*. Fran Tarkenton, the professional football player and later CEO of the Tarkenton Productivity Group, told Rowan that intuitives' inherent quality of risk taking may be their most important personality trait.

An acute sense of correct timing for acquisitions seemed to be the crucial factor in the successful career of Ted Turner of Turner Broadcasting System. And the quality of intuitive faith is well explained by Martina Horner, former president of Radcliffe College, who told Rowan, "You can't solve many of today's problems by straight linear thinking. It takes leaps of faith to sense the connections that are not necessarily obvious."[8]

Stephen Harper, who has written extensively on management and entrepreneurship, is also interested in the specific characteristics of top executives. Generalizing from his research, he notes:

> *Top executives seem to possess skills other managers lack. In addition to the usual managerial skills, they possess intuitive skills that provide them with different perspectives and different approaches for managing.... Top executives seem to blend their vision of the future with their intuitive skills when they venture forth into new industries, products and processes.*[9]

William Miller, author of *The Creative Edge: Fostering Innovation Where You Work*, identifies enthusiasm, risk tolerance and inner directedness as traits of successful intuitive business people.[10] Numerous thinkers and researchers have also noted that trust is an important personality trait of intuitive individuals.[11] And it appears that the key element of that trust is learning to trust your own intuitive information.[12]

As indicated by these and other researchers, the personality traits of those who are apt to experience and use their intuition are many and varied. Some traits are evidenced more in specialized areas, with particular people, under certain circumstances or at certain times. It has been found that people who are successful at using their intuition in business are apt to be:

- trusting of intuition
- self-confident
- comfortable with themselves
- open to criticism but not unduly swayed by others
- curious
- open to change in future possibilities
- comfortable with problem solving and challenges
- willing to take risks
- able to keep problem situations and possible solutions in mind

In addition, these individuals usually communicate honestly. They have a sense of correct timing that is associated with the appearance of their spontaneous ideas. They tend to perceive situations as a whole and easily see relationships among concepts. Rarely do they have trouble taking ambiguity into account when reviewing a problem. Overriding all of these traits is the firm belief in intuition itself.

"Follow your instincts. That's where true wisdom manifests itself."
—Oprah Winfrey, talk show host, entrepreneur and philanthropist

---

ENCOURAGING INTUITION IN THE WORKPLACE

In business, as in all parts of life, you can find many ways to encourage intuitive thoughts and insights. The suggestions that follow offer unique additions or compilations of approaches that can be used specifically in the business arena.

In his book, *Intuitive Management,* Weston Agor recommends

three components that encourage intuition in business. The first is the creation of an *environment* that allows intuition to function and flourish. He suggests that this should include office designs that allow for open communication, openness to informal attire in the workplace, flexible meeting agendas, cooperative problem solving and the encouragement of a healthy lifestyle.

The second component is the need to foster the *belief* in intuition as a viable tool in the work world. Agor suggests encouraging intuition in business by using the same methods that have proven successful in other settings. This includes meditation, imagery, self-hypnosis and the practice of non-judgment, non-projection and self-awareness.

The third component is the necessary encouragement of the *use and verification* of intuition. This involves teaching people to separate out ideas that come from the ego from those that come from the reality of intuition. Finally, in general terms, Agor relies upon Vaughan's and Goldberg's many suggestions for accessing and developing intuition that were previously noted.[13]

In his interviews with business leaders about their use of intuition, Rowan found that these leaders access their intuition in a variety of ways by

- walking around the office or plant to get a feel for the situation
- keeping the problem in mind
- redefining the problem
- considering the alternatives
- distinguishing between the real and imagined problems
- playing with analogies
- relaxing and letting the mind wander
- utilizing physical aids such as walking in nature, jogging and fasting
- utilizing dreamwork, biofeedback and meditation
- keeping an open mind
- having belief and faith in intuition

- visualizing a positive outcome
- letting go of the fear of failure
- trusting that the answer will arise
- being receptive to whatever comes, no matter how fleeting the intuition

After an intuition arrives, these business leaders recommend verifying the insight through analysis, listening to others, and journaling about the results. By consistently following these steps you can be more attuned to your intuition the next time around.

"I know when I have a problem and have done all I can to figure it out, I keep listening in a sort of inside silence until something clicks and I feel a right answer."
—Conrad Hilton, founder of Hilton Hotels

In *The Creative Edge*, William Miller suggests that we first look at the intuitive process as a continuous cycle that necessarily involves linear thought. To him, intense objective or linear modes must be used in the preparation stage to clarify and define the problem. This is followed by what many intuition researchers call an incubation period of letting go.[14] After this letting-go phase, the intuition appears. The intuitive cycle continues as the intuition is followed by a mental analysis, another incubation-type period, another intuition, another analysis and so on.

To generate new ideas, Miller uses analogies that spring from any source, whether personal, direct, symbolic or fantasy. For example, the inspiration for Velcro came from the analogy of the burdock burr. As do many of the other researchers, he also suggests using breathing exercises as well as imagery, brainstorming, dreamwork, drawing and meditation, with accompanying exercises, to help develop or enhance intuitive powers.[15]

Similar to Miller's use of analogies, Parikh et al. suggest that we use imagery to access intuition in our work lives. Whether you approach imagery passively or actively depends on your purpose. When searching for a general direction, you can approach imagery passively, letting images flow in when you are relaxed or in meditation. In this way you can develop receptivity while maintaining "choiceless awareness."

When you are seeking an answer to a specific question or choosing among alternatives you can use an active or deliberate approach. This approach calls for guided imagery, posing questions to a wise person or yourself as a detached other person and waiting to hear the response.

When you want to identify a correct alternative, imagine choosing an option and then ask yourself how that choice feels in your body, your mind, emotions and total self. When all of your parts are in agreement with an alternative, this indicates that you have found an authentic intuition.

Integrating Knowledge and Intuition

Michael Ray has outlined truths about successfully integrating intuition into the workplace. One truth is that "Intuition complements reason." This is an important point to remember when fear of intuition makes us think of it as being opposed to logic or reason. As Ray stated:

> *No one is suggesting that decisions should be made solely on the basis of intuition. It is the combination of experience, information, reason, and intuition that is so powerful.*[16]

In *Building a Knowledge-Based Culture*, authors Glenn Tecker, Kermit Eide, and Jean Frankel offer the useful concept of *informed intuition* to define this synthesis of reason and intuition within an organization:

> *When intelligently considered, defensible information is carefully blended with expert and user instincts about the future, and when this combination is consistently expected to be used in making decisions, the organization is operating with informed intuition.*[17]

The benefits that accrue from *informed intuition* can be maximized if a business or organization can move beyond the fear-based view of intuition as "hocus-pocus" and begin to value it as a legitimate and valuable source of day-to-day knowledge. As Ray notes: "People have to go beyond the idea... that [intuition] is the province of the gifted few or of oddballs."[18]

The role of intuition in business management has become one of the key issues in the ongoing debate about the skills most important for managers to have in the real world. This debate also involves the way in which business education programs prepare graduates for management. Henry Mintzberg, professor of management at McGill University's School of Business and a key player in this discussion, brought up the topic of intuition in his book, *The Rise and Fall of Strategic Planning*, to distinguish between "strategic planning" and "strategic thinking." He was quoted in the *Harvard Business Review* as stating that:

> *Strategic planning is not strategic thinking. Indeed, strategic planning often spoils strategic thinking, causing managers to confuse real vision with the manipulation of numbers. Strategic thinking is about synthesis. It involves intuition and creativity.*[19]

In his more recent book, *Managers Not MBAs*, Mintzberg again attempts to define a topic—management as a whole—by looking at what it is not, and in the process returns us to Ray's point about the necessary integration of intuition as an essential source of knowledge in business management. Under the subheading of "Management Is Not a Science," Mintzberg notes:

> *Science is about the development of systematic knowledge through research. That is hardly the purpose of management.... Management certainly applies science: managers have to use all the knowledge they can get, from the sciences and elsewhere. But management is more art, based on "insight," "vision," "intuition."*[20]

Some of our greatest business success stories in recent decades support Mintzberg's contentions. Scott Bedbury is an excellent example of this. He became known as the ultimate brand builder when he took Nike from being a relatively successful sneaker company to a sportswear superpower through his introduction of the now ubiquitous slogan, "Just Do It." A few years later he orchestrated Starbucks' stellar rise in the market, convincing the country that Starbucks is so essential to everyday living that we need one on every street corner.

In an interview published before Mintzberg's book, *Managers Not MBAs*, Bedbury discussed his views on the intrinsically intuitive nature of brand building in terms quite similar to Mintzberg's discussion of business management:

> *I've come to the conclusion that building a brand has more to do with art, more to do with the intangible aspects of running a company, than it does with the science or the tangible processes like finances or production or supply chain operations.... That's my problem with business books; they come out of the pre-quantification side. If you do that often enough, you forget what an idea feels like. The best ideas are felt, not measured.*[21]

While Bedbury is certainly an exceptional example, the truth is that we all have intuition. It is an ability with which we are born. Just as some of us have innately stronger sports or artistic abilities, some of us are born with a naturally easier access to our intuition. And just as we can improve our chess skills or golf games with practice, so can we use training and practice to improve our intuitive access and accuracy.

Research now demonstrates that intuition can help us to focus, see more options, broaden our awareness and improve our results. With increased confidence in our inner voice, we can see improvement in our personal and professional relationships, teamwork, planning, sales and other aspects of our personal and professional lives.

It probably is only the intuitive leap that will let us solve problems in this complex world. This is a major advantage of man over computer.
—Thomas Peters and Robert Waterman,
authors of *In Search of Excellence*

Review Questions

1. What is causing an increase in demand for intuition?

2. What are some key personality traits of successful intuitive business people?

3. How can management encourage intuition in the workplace?

4. What can you do to increase your intuition at work?

CHAPTER 9
INHIBITORS
OF INTUITION

*There is perhaps nothing so bad and so
dangerous in life as fear.*

**—Jawaharlal Nehru, first prime minister
of independent India**

Just as there are states of mind and traits of personality that support you in becoming more attuned to intuition, so are there those that inhibit the process. By identifying these inhibitors and taking informed action, you can move beyond these.

Fear of failure, fear of rejection and stress all inhibit your intuition. Being in a state of fear can block your reception, damage your interpretation and verification and interrupt accomplishing what you want. Therefore, by better understanding these inhibitors you can foster within yourself hopefulness, confidence, relaxation and faith in the potential for resolution.

FEAR: THE #1 INTUITION INHIBITOR

Fear is the strongest inhibitor of intuition.[1] It can stop your acceptance of an intuition and contaminate your interpretation of it when the truth is not the answer you want to hear. It can also serve as a defense mechanism whereby you rationalize that the intuition is wrong rather than accept its uncomfortable truth.[2] Fear can even cause you to deny an early warning signal of danger when you don't want to acknowledge a frightening yet intuitive truth.[3]

PHOBIAS

Extremely strong fears, such as phobias, can prevent you from receiving the correct information that is at hand. For example, when people have an unreasonable fear of flying, they don't know if they are receiving a true warning signal or simply experiencing their fear. For those with such phobias, all flights are draped in doom.[4]

FEAR AND WISHFUL THINKING

Both fear and desire can interfere with correctly acknowledging and/or interpreting your intuition.[5] You can block positive information coming in from your intuition when you incorrectly assume that your fear is actually your intuition. This is the opposite of wishful thinking.[6] With wishful thinking you assume that you are receiving positive intuitive information, whereas you are actually blocking unpleasant truths with personal desires.[7]

FEAR OF CENSURE

Fear of criticism, particularly in organizations and business, can stop you from acting upon your intuition when you lack the rational facts to comfortably back you up.[8] In 1960, Ray Kroc was one individual who conquered his fear of censure. He purchased the McDonald's name for $2.7 million against the advice of his attorneys. Yet, as he reported, "I felt in my funny bone it was a sure thing."[9] It could be said that he accessed universal truth with his intuition because, in less than twenty years, McDonald's sales topped $4.5 billion and today the golden arches can be seen worldwide.

FEAR OF FAILURE

Fear of failure and fear of making a mistake can stop you from listening to your intuition.[10] Fear of change and the fear of anything new—which signals a lack of confidence—can also interfere with your being able to hear your intuition. The fear of interpreting an intuition incorrectly can also contaminate the interpretation or cause you to reject the entire message. All of these fears are embodied in the fear of taking risks.

For example, when a loved one or close colleague is involved, fear of making a wrong interpretation can cause you to shy away from using your intuition. It is common to hesitate when depending upon your inner wisdom if there is the potential for affecting someone close to you. It is emotionally easier to play it safe and rely upon analytical information to solve the problem.[11]

FEAR OF REJECTION

In the West many people fear being thought of as impractical or non-rational which is equated with being less intelligent. This fear of not being respected, or being rejected, can prevent you from being willing to rely on your intuition.[12]

Regurgitating facts that you were told by authorities often feels safer and more comfortable.[13] It is usually harder to speak about the original messages you received from your intuition. But if you don't acknowledge the initial intuition, it can become buried by the desire to "think of everything" logically. Subsequently, the further flow of intuitive information is stymied.[14]

Often it can feel safer and easier to repress intuition through "non-recognition, devaluation... and neglect" than to embrace it.[15] At times you may have found yourself submerged in the continuous study of a problem, which created a situation of "paralysis by analysis." This can easily block your intuition.[16]

Krishnamurti put it this way: "Fear of not being, of not gaining, of not arriving," makes people compulsively grasp onto the status quo. It blocks your channels from being open to the goodness of the universe.[17] This lack of faith and trust in yourself blocks you from your intuitive wisdom.[18]

WARRANTED VERSUS UNWARRANTED FEAR FOR SURVIVAL

Interestingly enough, warranted fear for survival is not an inhibitor. Instead, your intuition encourages you to listen to the urgent signals of real danger. That fear is, therefore, intuition at work. Paying attention to intuitively based fear messages can protect you from harm, whereas doubting or denying those fear signals will inhibit your intuitive process. Unwarranted fear, however, is a product of the imagination and not your intuition.[19]

To tell the difference between warranted fear and unwarranted fear, you can evaluate the purity of your responses. For example, let's say that you usually take a walk through your neighborhood at night and rarely feel fear. Then one night intuition tells you to become more aware and you narrowly avert danger. You intuitively responded to a warranted fear. Now let's say that you were unaccustomed to walking outdoors after dark and became fearful at the prospect of doing so in your customarily safe neighborhood. This is, instead, unwarranted fear talking.

The good news is that you can actually train yourself to have more intuitive responses to situations. Through practicing, you can learn to recognize which fears are warranted and which are simply summoned by your imagination. As you review the outcomes of your experiences, you will begin to sense which information is initiated from your intuition. You may come to notice that when you are calm and then suddenly get a "hit" to become more aware, you are communicating with your intuitive wisdom.

THE MANY FACES OF NEGATIVITY

Taking yourself too seriously is another block to spontaneous flashes—while playfulness, in contrast, fosters them.[20] Negativity itself can stop you from trusting that you have intuitive abilities and keep you from having faith in your own wisdom.[21] In fact, any negative state of mind, such as anger, anxiety,[22] fatigue or depression, can also interfere with your awareness of subtle intuitive signals and distort your interpretations.[23]

In contrast, positive emotions between people facilitate the ability to communicate intuitively, particularly in instances where there are messages of danger and distress.[24] This is because positive emotions carry intuition better than negative emotions; in fact, they will open the floodgates to intuitive information.

For example, when your mind is stuck in a loop obsessing about someone you dislike, you most likely have no access to your intuitive faculties. Your negative emotions have blocked you from receiving information not only about the person you dislike but also about everything in general. Whereas when you are feeling happy and good about yourself and others, you can more easily receive intuitions about everything from the people you love to the world at large.

STRESS HURTS

When you are in a state of stress, tension, anxiety or frustration, it is difficult to contact your inner wisdom.[25] Even the stress of trying to be intuitive can interfere with the spontaneous occurrence of intuitive signals.[26] Denying or repressing incoming information can cause further inner turmoil in your life, which then intensifies the blockage in your intuitive system.[27]

Any form of stress or tension is the opposite of being relaxed, and experts agree that relaxation is necessary for the natural flow of intuition.[28] Individuals who are naturally quite intuitive often become stressed and therefore less open to the flow of information if they are watched while attempting to complete a task or when they are required to produce on demand.[29]

According to Yogananda, the static restlessness of the mind[30] or mental noise, a term used by many psychologists,[31] interferes with your reception. This interference can also be called mind-chatter. When you can't hear yourself think, it is hard to listen to your intuition.[32]

WHEN SELF-IMAGE GETS IN THE WAY

Your self-image can dramatically influence your intuitive abilities, whether you are positive and self-satisfied or negative and self-flagellating. Research has shown that having an unrealistic positive self-image can be just as inhibiting to intuition as being overly self-critical.

Identifying with an unrealistic positive self-image can block you from receiving insights about yourself that could assist you with your personal development. Such an unrealistic self-image can also interfere with correct interpretations of these insights. To fully receive the messages, people need to be open to seeing themselves more truthfully.[33] Those in positions of power, such as CEOs, must be especially alert to the possibility of faulty self-images or a misplaced self-confidence when using their intuition.[34]

An unrealistic negative self-image can also interfere with intuitive abilities. For example, when you are self-critical you doubt or disapprove of a part of yourself, thereby rejecting the fullness of your intuition.[35] Fear of success is a blocking emotion[36] that is especially found among women.[37] Through cultural conditioning some women have developed a self-image that allows them to hold onto passive and self-deprecating attitudes. This results in a general repression of intuitive skills.[38] Such attitudes can also be found as an end product of racial inequality.[39]

PREJUDGMENT

When you are emotionally connected to people, your intuition can be clouded in two ways. You can block intuitive information through prejudging them negatively. This is because you have prejudged them, or perhaps held onto an old judgment that is outdated, before you have actually received any current intuitive information about them. You can also block yourself from receiving information by imagining people more positively than they truly are. Often this is done in situations when people want someone to be the man or woman of their dreams. Wishful thinking can block the truth.

If, instead, you are lovingly connected to others and accept and see them for who they truly are, intuitive information can find a home within you. This is because you are not filtering or misinterpreting the information. Instead of being overly critical or unrealistically wishful, you are being realistic and open to what you can see.

PROJECTION

Projection is the unconscious process of attributing ideas and impulses to another. It can be confused with intuition and thereby stand in the way of authentic messages. When you unconsciously project onto another those qualities you do not recognize in yourself, be they positive or negative, you can easily misinterpret your projections to be intuitive information about the other person. Real intuitions are blocked by these projections. To open up to your intuition, you must instead recognize personal issues, be honest with yourself and take the position of inner witness.[40] In this way you can train yourself to identify the difference between the influence of personal issues and real intuitive insights.[41]

RIGIDITY AND PREJUDICE

Rigidity of character and prejudice can also stand in the way of your intuition. If you are rigid, dogmatic and have made up your mind, then you are not going to be open to new intuitive information.[42] Striving for consistency or control and fearing to take risks are other forms of rigidity.[43] Identifying with particular personal, cultural or religious prejudices and traditions can also strongly bias your interpretations.[44]

THE EDUCATIONAL SYSTEM

One final thought on the inhibitors of intuition is proposed by Henry Mintzberg, professor of management, and Fran Tarkenton of the Tarkenton Productivity Group. They found that business schools and business consultants were historically unsupportive of the intuitive process.[45] Roy Rowan, former writer for *Life, Time* and *Fortune*, agrees with this line of thinking.[46] Norman Shealy, neurosurgeon, university professor and founder of the American Holistic Medical Association, goes further by stating that, "On the whole the Western educational system is simply counterintuitive."[47]

Though there has been a significant suppression of intuition in the past, there now seems to be a movement, in some pockets, toward fostering it in education, business and related fields. Books on intuition are becoming more prevalent, and there are more intuitive business consultants being hired today than ever before.

REVIEW QUESTIONS

1. How does fear keep you from accessing your intuition?

2. What other conditions potentially inhibit your intuition?

3. When has stress negatively affected your intuition?

4. How can an unrealistic self-image affect your intuition?

CHAPTER 10
THE BASIS FOR THE EUREKA! SYSTEM

You must train your intuition—you must trust the small voice inside you that tells you exactly what to say, what to decide.

—Ingrid Bergman, Oscar-winning actress

One of the first twentieth-century writers who discussed the processes of thought was Graham Wallas, a British psychologist. In his 1926 landmark book, *The Art of Thought*, he outlined the four stages of "thought processes." Over the years his well-defined stages were adopted by researchers in the fields of creativity and intuition to frame their new ideas and systems. Following are his stages and related ideas of those who have followed him in their research. Wallas and his successors represent the intellectual foundation for the *Eureka! System*, which is laid out for you in the chapters to come.

WALLAS' FOUR STAGES OF THOUGHT

The four stages of thought processes proposed by Graham Wallas are *preparation, incubation, illumination* and *verification*.[1] These overlap one another. Wallas' *preparation* stage, the necessary foundation for an intuitive experience, involves analytically formulating a question and becoming familiar with the topic through research.[2] This allows you to more easily identify an intuition when it is later received. Familiarity with a topic is the reason so many people are able to receive more intuitions in their fields of expertise.

Following preparation is the *incubation* period when you let go of previously held conscious consideration on your topic. Wallas suggests that during incubation you "consciously arrange either to think on other subjects than the proposed problem or to rest from any form of conscious thought."[3]

Illumination, the third component, refers to the moment of the intuitive flash. And, finally, the *verification* stage involves the process of discovering the truth about the experience.[4]

STAGE 1: PREPARATION

During Wallas' *preparation* stage of information gathering, people usually approach their unanswered questions and problems in a rational manner. They gather all information possible and use their logic to search for solutions.

In addition to this rational approach, Milton Fisher, teacher of applied creativity and author of the book, *Intuition: How to Use It for Success and Happiness*, recommends *judgment deferral* exercises that can be practiced by yourself. These follow the principles of *brainstorming* in which ideas flow freely and immediately, thereby accessing your intuitive mind while bypassing your analytical mind. During these exercises you postpone all judgment.[5]

In the initial phase of what Goldberg has devised as a two-part incubation period, you direct a question to your intuition. The question should be precise while allowing for complex and/or unexpected answers.[6] You may find it helpful to write down random thoughts about the situation and finish sentences such as, "I have a feeling that..." and "What I don't know is...." You can also draw, paint, sculpt, create a symbol, sing, dance, or play on a musical instrument to further express the situation in question. Brainstorming, either with others or alone, can also be very useful at this time.[7]

STAGE 2: INCUBATION

If no answer is forthcoming in the *preparation* stage, then many researchers believe that you then consciously or unconsciously lapse into a period of *incubation*.[8] You can expect an answer to appear here or at some later date. If an answer did appear during the *preparation* stage, and you still want more clarity, then more intuitions might arise in this *incubation* stage. Under any circumstance, it is during this time that the problem is put aside.[9]

During *incubation* you let go of the relevant issues and go about your daily routines. You can engage in meditation, physical and mental relaxation, daydreams, night dreams, hypnosis or play. This time could also include reading on other subjects but should not include passive reading on the topic under your consideration.[10]

Just as withdrawing from the mundane world for a time and letting go of the issue is key to Wallas' second stage, so is it key to the second half of Goldberg's *incubation* period. This is a significant time. Many archetypal figures, who turn away from the world and return with renewed strength and wisdom, are woven into our ancient folklore, mythology and literature. Joseph Campbell in his book, *The Hero with a Thousand Faces*, gives us the story of the hero's journey through separation, initiation and return. In the initiation phase he connects with a higher power, learning what he needs to know, so that he can make his eventual return as a changed person. During this time of initiation or *incubation* Moses, Jesus, Buddha and other spiritual figures are believed to have communed with the divine.[11]

Tools that have been recommended by many for use during this period include *meditation, relaxation exercises, imagery* and *dreamwork*.[12] Fisher recommends *self-hypnosis* for relaxation because it increases your receptivity to intuition. As he explains it, self-hypnosis relaxes the conscious mind, thereby eliminating mind-chatter and letting the intuitive mind become more dominant.[13]

One story of releasing problems and turning them over to the unconscious mind involves the successful financier J. P. Morgan. When faced with a difficult problem, he would relax by playing the game of solitaire for an hour. Following this, the correct decision would intuitively come to him.[14]

William James, the philosopher, linked relaxation and release with intuition just as did many philosophers, psychologists and business people following him. Experience taught him how to enhance his intuitive abilities. He valued intuition as a type of religious experience:

> *The way to success... is by... surrender... passivity, not activity; relaxation, not intentness.... Give up the feeling of responsibility, let go your hold, resign the care of your destiny to higher powers, be genuinely indifferent as to what becomes*

of it all and you will find... a perfect inward relief.... By relaxing, letting go... [you will give] your little private convulsive self a rest... finding that a greater Self is there.[15]

STAGE 3: ILLUMINATION

An intuition may emerge in the form of an image, word or emotion at any time during *incubation*. During the *illumination* stage, you allow the intuition to appear in a natural form by acting as a neutral spectator who observes the occurrence.[16] You can assist yourself in this effort by preparing yourself to withhold rational judgment at the onset of your flash.[17]

André Marie Ampère, the French mathematician and physicist for whom the unit of electrical current was named, gives us a clear example of *illumination* that comes as the result of going through the *preparation* and *incubation* stages. He records his excitement in his diary as follows:

I gave a shout of joy.... It was seven years ago I proposed to myself a problem which I have not been able to solve directly, but for which I had found by chance a solution, and knew that it was correct, without being able to prove it. The matter often returned to my mind and I had sought twenty times unsuccessfully for this solution. For some days I had carried the idea about with me continually. At last, I do not know how, I found it, together with a large number of curious and new considerations concerning the theory of probability.[18]

STAGE 4: VERIFICATION

Once you have received your *intuition*, then you move into Wallas' *verification* stage. Goldberg gives this final stage the title of *validation*. In this stage you determine whether an intuition is worth acting upon. Self-awareness and an expanded state of consciousness can help you in preventing errors when validating intuitive information. As Goldberg explains, "If you are observant, you will gradually acquire sensitivity to your patterns of interaction with intuition, and if any psychological factors are standing in the way, they will be revealed."[19]

Begin by applying objective analysis to those intuitions you consider to be valid and worthy of further discovery. Keep analytically reinterpreting the data and evaluating each questionable interpretation. If desired, you can then encourage a series of additional insights about your analysis. Tony Bastick titles this combined process "intuitively guided analysis."[20]

An example of someone who uses additional intuitions to *verify* an initial intuition is provided by Rosanoff. This may seem like a circular and illogical process to rational thinkers, but this is a useful approach for validation. As she notes,

> *A friend of mine is a forensic accountant. He is brought into situations as a detective, looking for accounting errors and determining criminal intent. He shared with me his process, as follows: Immediately upon opening the books a feeling comes over him. Something feels fishy about these books— he knows something is wrong but he doesn't know what. He keeps looking and looking until he finds something, then there may or may not be an "aha" feeling of "that's it!" If there is the feeling, he knows he has found the major problem. If there is no feeling, then he knows he has to keep looking. Intuition has validated itself with an intuitive feeling. It begins with a feeling and is verified with a feeling.*[21]

Goldberg recommends that you keep an "intuition journal" to record information about each of your occurrences, including both the successful and the incorrect outcomes of all previously assumed intuitions.[22] Vaughan also notes that journal keeping can be an important tool in learning how to distinguish between verifiable intuitions and wishful thinking.[23] By writing down your intuitions in one place, you can easily go back to your notes and verify which were intuitions and which were not.

Keeping a more elaborate "intuitive diary," in which you record information in three columns, is Fisher's suggestion. In the first column, define the problem as a factual story, leaving out any judgments. In the second column, review the same event from a relaxed and larger perspective, using the intuitive mind. In the third column, record the outcome of the intuitive message a few days or weeks later. This diary satisfies the multiple purposes of observing, increasing, interpreting and verifying intuitions.[24]

The Stages of Creativity

Gardner Murphy, who wrote *Human Potentialities* thirty years after Wallas published his work, specifically focuses on the topic of creativity. He describes four phases or stages that are necessary in the creative process, which can be extended to the processes of intuition. In the first stage you immerse yourself in a specific area of interest. Next you accumulate experiences and unconsciously organize and incubate them in your mind. This results in the third stage to which he gives a variety of names: *inspiration, illumination* and *insight*. The final stage involves "sifting and testing, the critical evaluating and perfecting of the work done."[25]

Willis Harman and Howard Rheingold, in their book, *Higher Creativity: Liberating the Unconscious for Breakthrough Insights*, explore "breakthrough experiences." They refer to these experiences as "creativity, inspiration, poetic imagination, intuition, mediumship and revelation"[26] Even though they mainly use the term "higher creativity," they are addressing what we have discussed as intuition.

Expanding upon Wallas' four components, they add subtitles using computer terminology. Preparation is titled the *input mode* in which you become intellectually informed on a topic while emotionally concentrating upon it.[27] The questions you formulate during this time are then, "clearly, completely, and intently... directed to the unconscious." The composer Richard Strauss stated something similar. He wrote,

> *I can tell you from my own experience that an ardent desire and fixed purpose combined with intense inner resolve brings results. Determined concentrated thought is a tremendous force.*[28]

Once you have completed the *input mode* you move into the *processing mode*, which is similar to Wallas' second stage of *incubation*. Here you shift from a state of concentration to one in which you relax your conscious mind. To Wallas' list of diversions for this stage, Harman and Rheingold add the idea of very consciously turning your problem over to your unconscious mind so that you can let go and forget about it. Next, in the *output mode*, which Wallas titles *illumination*, you let your unconscious ideas flow freely. And finally, the *verification* stage is the same.[29]

PROBLEM-SOLVING STAGES

Eugene Gendlin, the humanistic psychologist and author of *Focusing*, does not use the word intuition, but he does suggest a means for problem solving that is similar to some of the intuitive systems previously mentioned. He offers no designated period for incubation although his process does require deliberate relaxation and letting go within the body. In focusing you sit quietly (but not in meditation or necessarily alone), pose a question, suggest possible solutions and then notice your physical reactions, bodily shifts, mental symbols and words. You check all of these reactions in the next round of intuitions, making this a series of verifications. You then repeat these steps until you find resolution.

INTUITION PROCESSES

Frances Vaughan, author of *Awakening Intuition*, reviews three steps for increasing access to intuition. *Quieting the mind* is her first step, which can include meditation and relaxation exercises. *Focused attention* or concentration is the second step, and the third and final step involves *receptivity* to intuition, which requires developing a non-judgmental attitude.

Philip Goldberg in his book, *The Intuitive Edge*, lists a three-stage process for accessing *intuition*. He groups Wallas' first two components of the thought process, *preparation* and *incubation*, into an inclusive phase that he calls *incubation*. Following his *intuition* stage is the final stage, which he names *validation*.

Marcia Emery, in *Intuition Workbook*, outlines an eight-step system she titles *Intuition Problem-Solving (IPS)*. This includes (1) defining your *problem* in the form of a question; (2) *centering* yourself through listening to music, saying affirmations or using focusing techniques; (3) increasing your *receptivity* to intuition through breathing or relaxation techniques; (4) *eliciting imagery* (intuition) passively through receiving a flash or actively through applying techniques; (5) *interpreting the imagery;* (6) *resting;* (7) *further interpreting* the imagery using new insights; and finally (8) *activating the solution.*

As you can see, many systems build upon the initial ideas of Wallas.

REVIEW QUESTIONS

1. What are Wallas' four stages of thought?

2. What ways could you spend time in the incubation stage?

3. When might an intuition appear?

4. What is the value in keeping an intuition journal?

PART 3

The *Eureka! System* for Accessing Intuition

In the next fifty to one hundred years, we will see our society changed by psi-related, intuitive technologies at least as much as automobiles and computers have already changed our civilization.

—Jeffrey Mishlove, former director of the Intuition Network

By following the steps on the pages to come, and reading the illustrative examples and stories, you can learn the *Eureka! System*. This is an easy, flexible and reliable method for accessing your intuition, especially in decision making. My purpose in developing this was to give you seven simple steps to follow, in all situations—normal and stressful—so you can feel confident when using your intuitive abilities.

- Chapter 11 – You learn the *Eureka! System*—in which you *ACT and LEAP!*—through explanations and examples.

- Chapter 12 – You learn, through stories, how to hone your intuitive skills. You then discover how many ways intuition can appear in your life. Next, you become knowledgeable at identifying when another's claim of intuition is really an intuition. Finally, "Can you trust your intuition?"

CHAPTER 11

THE *EUREKA!* SYSTEM: SEVEN STEPS TO INTUITION

> *The will can encourage the intuitive operation by formulating questions to... the intuition.... The replies may come promptly, but more often they appear after a lapse of time and when least expected.*
>
> **—Roberto Assagioli, psychoanalyst who developed psychosynthesis**

Wallas' four stages of thought have long served as a valuable basis for further consideration and research for so many of us. Yet over the years clients have asked me, "When do I use intuitive tools to increase my intuition? Where do they fit into the four stages?" These questions and others spurred me and Greg Meyerhoff on to develop the *Eureka! System*, which incorporates three additional steps to give you a solid structure for your understanding. These seven steps satisfy your analytical mind while allowing for the fluidity inherent in the intuitive process.

USING THE SEVEN STEP SYSTEM

This system assists you in navigating the course to your chosen destination. Your destination could be an answer to a question or a solution to a problem that has been troubling you. Depending upon the issue, you could take the steps in order, change their order, skip steps or repeat them.

For example, let's say that you want to cross a mountain stream. You make your way across, stepping on every successive stone. The next time you cross, the water is lower and you decide to skip some stones. Another time, you choose to jump from one stone to the next and back again to gain some stability before moving ahead. Still other times, you choose to go back to the original bank and cross the stream again to become more completely satisfied with your journey. No matter how you cross the stream, your intuition can appear at any time.

ACT AND LEAP!

With the *Eureka! System* you can use the mnemonic device, or memory aid, of A-C-T and L-E-A-P to remember the seven steps for accessing intuition:

Step 1:	**A**sk for what you want
Step 2:	**C**larify your desire
Step 3:	Use **T**ools
Step 4:	**L**et go
Step 5:	**E**ureka!
Step 6:	**A**ct on *Eureka!*
Step 7:	**P**rove it

STEP 1: ASK

To get what you want, you must first ask the universe, via your intuition, to bring it to you. This is not a time to be shy. To activate this process you need an initial spark of desire.

Thoughts and desires can float around in your head all day long even though you may not be aware of them. Most people continuously make requests of their intuition and create with their thoughts without being consciously aware of doing so. Without realizing it, you could spend all of your time asking for things that aren't that important to you. You could also unknowingly block your intuitive abilities when you judge yourself with an internal comment such as, "That was stupid of me."

By bringing your positive desires more into conscious awareness in this *asking step,* you open up the channels of intuition and invite a partnership with your inner wisdom. What exactly do you desire? What questions do you want answered? What insights do you want in life? It is time to state what you think you want and *ask* for answers. You can then expect the intuitive solution to come to you.

EXAMPLE OF STEP *1: ASK*

To give you an example of *Step 1,* let us say that until now you have been happy with your car, but at this point you feel you would like a new one. You realize that there may be many reasons behind wanting a new car. So you ask your analytical mind, "Why do I want a new car?" You also ask your intuitive mind, "What is the real (hidden) reason behind my wanting a new car? Would it be really good for me?"

You *ask* to have your desire fulfilled. You put your request for answers out into the ethers. Willingly now, you go through the following steps to discover what is behind your desire for a new car.

STEP 2: CLARIFY

Now it is time to *clarify* what you want because that will increase the odds of your journey being a successful one. This *clarifying step* involves using both your rational and intuitive minds to examine your desire and/or question. In this way you can determine if what you think you want is right for you.

Assuming you want an answer to a question or a solution to a problem, you now explore the issue on a mental, physical, emotional and spiritual level. You employ:

- questioning others: What do other people say?
- mental analysis: What does your research tell you?
- physical sensations: What does your body tell you?
- emotional feedback: What do your emotions tell you?
- spiritual questioning: What do you find and learn in meditation and self-hypnosis?

• environmental information: What do your physical
surroundings tell you?

If you use only your analytical mind to gather facts and learn about
your particular issue or situation, it is easy for your rational mind
to want to take over the process. You could immobilize yourself looking for answers that you feel must be somehow buried in the facts. The
old trap of "paralysis by analysis" could keep you stuck in *Step 2* for
a long time.

To remedy this paralysis, you can add an intuitive inquiry to the
mix. This helps you become more balanced in your search and gives
you more information. If you feel that your intuitive mind is not accessible enough to you as yet, or that the information you are receiving is
somehow polluted, then simply take a mental note of that. It could be
that a "clean" intuition is something you want to ask for in *Step 1* in
the future. You can also use the techniques in *Step 3*, the *tools step*, to
become more generally intuitive.

In clarifying what you want, you may decide to redefine your desire or alter your request in some way. This is the perfect time to do that.
Remember, "Ask and you shall receive." A well-defined picture of what
you desire to create insures a good outcome.

EXAMPLE OF STEP 2: CLARIFY

If you want a new car and want to know why you have that desire,
it is now time to *clarify* your questions through researching the possibilities. Your friends, the Internet and *Consumer Reports* give you a
lot of good information. Armed with all of this, you head to the dealer-
ships to test-drive your favorite models. You find that your body reacts
the best to the most expensive cars, and, emotionally, you feel you
deserve one of them. But you know that you could use the help of some
intuitive tools to both clear your mind and receive some imagery from
your intuition. You wait to make your decision until after you have applied some tools and have clearer access to your intuition.

STEP 3: TOOLS

In the *using tools step*, you engage in activities and practice techniques that help you increase your access to intuition. This step may well lead to your answers. Some techniques, such as brainstorming, primarily help you find immediate answers while other practices, such as meditation, self-hypnosis and dreamwork, help you increase your receptivity to intuition overall. You can also apply some tools, such as brainstorming and self-hypnosis, in *Step 2* to gain some clarity. (See Chapters 13, 14, 15, 16 for details.)

During the *tools step*, you want to remain open to any and all answers, trusting that the best answer will appear at the appropriate time. You might also want to take some time now to become familiar with the traits that are attributed to intuitive people. Are there some traits that you would like to acquire? What might be some inhibitors to your intuitive process? (See Chapters 7, 8, 9.)

In preparing to receive your intuition, you want to become more self-aware and as clear of ego contamination and judgment as possible. You also want to do what you can to become receptive physically, emotionally, mentally and spiritually. This can be accomplished through a variety of activities:

- exercise and a clean diet
- reading stimulating and inspiring works
- hypnotherapy and psychotherapy
- meditation and spiritual practices

EXAMPLE OF STEP 3: TOOLS

After you meditate, thereby clearing your mind of the mental noise, you feel much better but are still not sure which car is right for you. However, now, without all of the salespeople's chatter in your head, you are ready to go inside using the tool of self-hypnosis to see an image of the best overall car for you. Your intuitive mind brings you an image of a less expensive car. You know this is not wishful thinking because you originally saw yourself in the most expensive car on the lot. You joke to yourself that psychotherapists could make a fortune off of you.

With this happy attitude, you head back to the dealership and again test-drive the car you saw in your intuitive imagery. You find that you feel comfortable both physically and emotionally sitting behind the wheel of that car. It satisfies your mind to know that with the purchase of this car you can put the money you are saving toward other interests. You purchase the car and feel good.

STEP 4: LET GO

(To proceed with *Step 4*, imagine now that there was no resolution in *Step 3*.)

If you are feeling exhausted, and frustrated that your intuition has not yet spoken to you, it is time to move on to *Step 4* and completely *let go*. In the *letting go step*, you put the question aside, return to your daily routine and turn your attention to other subjects. You neither dwell on, nor continue to look into, your present question or problem.

You can always practice meditation or a good relaxation program as long as you release the focus from your desire and refocus on letting go and relaxing. This is a good time to:

- read on a completely different subject
- exercise for pure pleasure
- take a walk or spend time in nature
- engage in your favorite pastime
- listen to enjoyable music
- talk to animals
- sleep and enjoy dreamtime
- laugh and have fun

Just as with any of the previous steps, it is possible that an insight may appear unexpectedly here as well. It could happen while taking a walk or perhaps be triggered by someone's chance remark. You may also discover your answer through dream journaling, which makes the information you receive through dreams more accessible to you.

It is from this state of being open to receiving the answer, rather than pursuing the answer, that an intuitive flash or insight can spring. This period might last for a short time or extend into years. It is important to keep your mind open to receiving intuitions during all of your activities throughout this *letting go step*.

EXAMPLE OF STEP 4: LET GO

Let us say once again that in *Step 3: Tools*, while you were in self-hypnosis, you received and accepted the image of a less expensive car. This time, however, when you returned to the dealership and took it for another test drive, you rejected it. Nothing felt right and you don't know what to do. You assume that you were unable to relax enough to fully contact your intuition when you were practicing self-hypnosis. Your mind had been contaminated by the strong desire to have an immediate answer. This caused the information you received to be incomplete or perhaps faulty.

You would like to revisit the *tools* and enter self-hypnosis once again, but you recognize that the stresses of daily life have overcome you. You give up the search and forget about buying a new car for now. You decide to spend your money on a nice trip where you can simply relax. You call your travel agent and book a beach vacation.

STEP 5: *EUREKA!*

Eureka! An intuitive flash appears in your consciousness! What excitement and relief. The whole world takes on a rosy glow. You have done your homework and fully deserve to receive this information. You have just experienced the *Eureka! step*.

Intuitive insights can be received through a variety of modes—visual images and symbols, verbal messages, emotional feelings, physical sensations or environmental cues—or you might just have an immediate idea or general sense of knowing. One mode of reception is just as valuable as another. With practice you can receive insights through more than one preferred mode.

The messages you receive may have meaning only for you. For example, you may unexpectedly come across a sentence in a book or hear a song that answers your question. You may have a sudden gut feeling or an emotional response to a topic. You may receive an unexpected phone call that provides you with your answer, or feel an immediate overall sense of knowing while in the shower.

When the *Eureka!* moment comes to you, you can choose to end the process at this point or further refine your question and let your intuitive mind bring you additional information. This can be an ongoing process that allows you to refocus and add questions as you continue to seek more insights.

EXAMPLE OF STEP 5: EUREKA!

You take your vacation and find that the time at the beach is very good for you. Long walks, sleeping in, playing your favorite sports, enjoying the beautiful views and watching funny movies lets you feel like yourself again. While you are relaxing, you find yourself reviewing your life. You realize that your car is really not the problem. *Eureka!* Sure, a new car would make you feel better, but the real issue is your job. It is no longer satisfying to you—it has become dull over time. A new car would be a feel-good distraction for a while but not the answer in the long run.

STEP 6: ACT

In the *acting step*, you take action on what you believe to be your intuition. This action can bring you proof as to whether you imagined, or actually received, an intuition. For example, let's say that you are taking a walk on a bike path; you look both ways, see no one coming and decide to stride down the middle for a while. After a few carefree minutes, you suddenly feel that you should move to your correct right side of the path and do so. Suddenly, a racing biker appears out of the blue and rushes past you. You later reflect on how you took action and then received immediate proof that it was truly your intuition at work for you.

There are definitely occasions when you have to make such quick decisions to take action. But there are many other times when it is more appropriate to move on to *Step 7* and prove that it was an intuition before you make such a move.

EXAMPLE OF STEP 6: ACT

When you get back from your vacation, you find a message on your voicemail from a former classmate with whom you have kept in touch sporadically over the years. He was thinking about you and wondered if you might be interested in coming to work for his company. You are amazed at this synchronicity! You take *action* by calling him back to set up a time to meet and discuss the position. (You are taking an *action* without making a total commitment.)

Before going to the meeting, you ask yourself the question, "Is this job right for me?" In other words, you take yourself back to *Step 1: Ask.* You then proceed to *Step 2: Clarify,* and do your homework by calling around and researching the industry. You find that his company is solid and that your skill set fits the job description. When you find a flattering article on the Internet about the company, a good feeling suddenly comes over you letting you know that something is right. You are having another *Eureka!* moment. So you *act* once again by committing to yourself that you will proceed in a positive manner.

In the negotiations, everything sounds good and the salary offer is an improvement over your present job. But you still aren't sure, so you tell him you want to sleep on it. (In this way, you are taking additional *action.*)

STEP 7: PROVE

In this *proving step* you confirm or deny the information you were given in your *Eureka!* moment. Was your flash a "real intuition?" Through words, imagery, symbols, emotions or bodily reactions, you now mentally analyze and intuitively sense the authenticity of the potential intuition that you received.

It's wise to take a moment to check in with your intuitive sense of knowing to determine whether it is truly an intuition or, instead, for example, an ego-induced fearful or wishful thought. You want to acknowledge and act upon *true* intuitions. Through practice you learn to use your intuition to distinguish thoughts or feelings derived from your ego from those derived from your intuition. If your body and mind, which together interpret your information, are too impure, then you may not be able to completely receive or correctly interpret the intuition. With such an acknowledgment you can choose to spend more time in the *tools step.*

Does the information in the intuitive flash fully solve your problem or answer your question? If not, go back to the *asking step* and ask once again for what you want, now that you have clarified it. Then proceed once more through the *clarifying, tools* and *letting go steps.* It could also be that you only need to practice a few chosen techniques from the *tools step* to proceed. In this way you are preparing yourself for another insight to clarify the previous message.

You are using your intuitive mind to interpret the meaning of the first intuition while you are also using it to validate the appearance of another *Eureka!* moment. You participate in this repetitive and circular process until you become satisfied with the validity of your possible intuitions. Ultimately, you may accept an intuition because you feel it is true, even though it may not be the answer you either expected or wanted.

An unexpected event or situation might confirm or contradict the flash. Imagery received through dreams that occur following an intuitive flash can also assist you in testing for validity. In any event, *proving* can be immediate or it may continue over time.

Because of intuition's elusive quality, it is helpful to immediately note your intuitive insights in a journal, along with the pertinent events surrounding it. You can also ask yourself, "What were my thoughts and feelings throughout this process? What were my clues? What did I learn about myself?" Through the process of documentation you can solidify within yourself the acceptance of these occurrences of intuition. The practice of journaling trains your analytical and intuitive minds to work together in this discovery process. It also increases the likelihood of your having more *Eureka!* moments in the future. Keeping a journal gives you the added benefit of having one place to return to where you can study your intuitions for successes and misses and areas of needed improvement.

EXAMPLE OF STEP 7: PROVE

After sleeping on your decision, you wake up the next morning feeling good about the job, but you would really like a sign to move ahead. You know that your intuition was right about not buying the car because you first needed to focus on your job situation. You now have proof of that. But you still want to know if your intuition is telling you to take this particular job or if it is only wishful thinking telling you that it will make your life easier. If all you are doing is changing companies, then you don't want to make the move.

As you have breakfast, the phone rings. It is your former classmate who has offered you the job saying, "If you haven't made up your mind yet, the job comes with a company car." You thank him and smile ear to ear. Now you have proof that this was your intuition speaking and providing you with the right decision.

REVIEW QUESTIONS

1. What are the seven steps of the *Eureka! System?*

2. What question do you have for your intuition? Use *ACT and LEAP!* to receive an answer.

3. What situation would you like solved by your intuition? Use *ACT and LEAP!* to bring you a solution.

CHAPTER 12

IDENTIFYING
EUREKA!

*When you force solutions on problems, you only create
new problems. But when you put your attention on the
uncertainty, and you witness the uncertainty while you
expectantly wait for the solution to emerge out of the chaos
and the confusion, then what emerges is something
very fabulous and exciting.*

**—Deepak Chopra, M.D., founder of
Chopra Center for Well Being**

Attending to your intuition with fresh eyes and objective
ears can be a lifelong endeavor that you pursue on a daily
basis. The *Eureka! System* gives you the means by which you
can eventually achieve these goals. The following stories, about
the appearances of intuition and the ways in which they might be
proven, can help you identify and trust your intuition.

IN PURSUIT OF PROOF: 5 SCENARIOS

Using relationship scenarios, these examples illustrate the
ways in which you can reflect upon the *proving step.* You can
see how individuals apply intuitive insights to the best of their
abilities. They attempt to analyze situations rationally *and* intuitively, and then reflect upon their abilities to read a situation.
If these same individuals were to learn about the intuitive process
and study the *Eureka System!* they would find it easier to identify
and understand the signals that they are receiving.

Scenario #1: A Series of Intuitions Achieves Success

A woman who has not gone out for a while is invited to a party. Her immediate intuitive response is to go, even though she had planned to complete a project that night which was due the following day. She wants to know if her "hit" to go is a true intuition or, instead, wishful thinking telling her that she might meet a good man there. She therefore mentally analyzes the work she has to do to see if she can actually get it done early the next morning. She determines that, with some difficulty, she can. She decides that, even though in the past she has used her work as an excuse to turn down invitations, this time it feels really important to go.

At the party she meets an interesting man and has the "feel good" intuition to accept a date from him. In her mind she counts this as her second intuition. During the week preceding the date, however, doubt creeps in and she questions her decision—she really doesn't know him at all. She keeps checking in with her intuitive feelings and still feels good about the date. But to satisfy her analytical mind she calls a mutual friend who says that he deserves a thumbs-up. Given all of this intuitive and analytical information, she decides to take action: she follows through and goes out on the date. She has a great time, and they make plans to get together again.

To review the process she went through, we note that she first carefully listened to what she assumed was an intuition and then verified it analytically and intuitively. She found that she did quite well and was pleased with her outcome—she had received two genuine and positive intuitions. She decided to remember this process mentally, emotionally and physically and let it sink into her bones so that she can repeat her success with intuition in the future.

Scenario #2: Experiencing Unwarranted Fear and Walking Through It

In the next example, a woman who has not dated in a while finds herself at a party and accepts a date from someone she meets there. The following morning she wakes up with a sick feeling in her stomach that she has made a mistake. In the days that follow she has disturbing thoughts about the upcoming date and criticizes herself harshly for saying that she would go out with this man. She thinks this is her intuition warning her of a rough road ahead.

Then the words of her former therapist start ringing in her ears, "Feel the fear and do it anyway." She has to decide whether the fear she was feeling was her intuition talking to her, or was she was simply fearful about reentering the dating scene, given her bad track record? She has the brilliant idea to move the date from dinner at an unfamiliar location to lunch at her favorite restaurant so there is less risk involved.

Because she is still confused and unable to determine which message is coming directly from her intuition and which one she might be misinterpreting, she decides to move ahead cautiously and goes out on the date. To her surprise, it is a great success, and she realizes that her initial intuition to accept the date has now been validated. Her later feeling of fear was proven to be not an intuition at all. She learned what it feels like to feel unwarranted fear, and she hopes that she will remember these thoughts and feelings so that she can walk through the next situation with more ease. She now knows that, at times, her intuition will be giving her new messages and opportunities to move through her old fears with appropriate caution.

SCENARIO #3: EXPERIENCING TRUE WARNINGS AND VALIDATING THEM IN REVIEW

Another woman has an intuitive feeling to go to the same party and finds herself attracted to an elusive man standing alone in the corner. She accepts a date with him and looks forward to seeing him later that week. As the week progresses something just doesn't feel right. She can't put her finger on it, but something feels off every time she thinks of him. She takes note of this gut feeling even though she doesn't know what it means.

On the date he casually mentions that he is separated from his wife. Now she knows why she had that uneasy feeling—her physical body was attracted to him, but she had previously made up her mind not to see anyone who was that unavailable. When she had dated men under these circumstances in the past, she had been hurt. She acknowledges that her physical body had given her one message of attraction while her gut feeling had given her the warning signal to cancel the date. In reviewing the situation she now knows what it feels like to get a real message of warranted fear. She is now more determined to keep listening to her intuition in the future.

SCENARIO #4: REVISITING THE MEANING OF AN INTUITION

A woman who has been really stressed out at work is thrilled when she receives an invitation to go to a party. As she thinks about the party, she has the strange feeling that she will be meeting someone important there with whom she could possibly share the rest of her life. She has listened to her intuition before and recognizes the signs. When she arrives at the party she mingles for quite a while and then gets down to the project at hand. She looks about the room and her eyes land on the man she thinks she is supposed to meet. After a long conversation with him, she doesn't get the hit that he is the one, but she still accepts a date. She goes home confused.

Over the next few weeks, she goes out with this man a variety of times and tries to make herself feel that feeling she has felt in previously good situations. But it just doesn't happen for her. At this same time, she starts up a new friendship with one of the women she also met at the party. Oddly, they soon feel almost like sisters even though they have known each other only a short time.

In reviewing this last couple of months, she realizes that her intuition was right about going to the party, but she had misinterpreted the message. The mental stress she had been under at work disrupted her ability to interpret her intuition properly. Yes, she was meant to go to the party to meet someone really important, but it wasn't a man. Instead, she was meant to meet a potentially good friend for life. She laughs at herself. She acknowledges that her intuition was strong and promises herself to be more open to its actual message next time.

SCENARIO #5: LISTENING TO WISHFUL THINKING AND LEARNING FROM THE EXPERIENCE

In this example, a woman goes to a party hoping to meet that special someone. She feels that tonight might be the night because so many synchronicities led up to that evening. Besides, everybody has been telling her that she will meet someone soon, and she believes them. As the evening progresses she talks to a man about getting together and they exchange numbers.

Anticipating an exciting relationship, she calls him later that week for a date and he declines. She is devastated and confused, thinking that her intuition has lied to her. What she doesn't see is that her wishful thinking about that man clouded her interpretation of the events. You could say she had been "out in left field" about everything.

For the time being she decides to give up her wishful thinking, which she had misinterpreted as intuition, and ends up attending the next party with no expectations. She is relaxed. When she suddenly has the impulse to turn around and talk to the person behind her, she does so without even thinking. Happily, they find each other to be attractive and later commence dating.

In retrospect, she realizes that her wishful thinking had distorted her interpretation of the first situation. Given this new understanding, she commits to making a practice of seeing the difference between projecting her desires and receiving valid information. After mentally reviewing the facts surrounding the second party, she validates her intuition that told her to turn around. She decides to be relaxed and let go of her previous need to force things to happen. She commits to listening to her intuition more in the future.

THE THREE APPEARANCES OF INTUITION

As you can see in the above scenarios, the occurrence of intuition can be experienced in a variety of ways. It appears at different times, and it comes either by surprise or by request. The appearances of intuitions have been categorized as *day-by-day* and *real spiritual*.[1] You could say that everyday intuitions show up both as un-requested flashes and as flashes in response to conscious requests. Sublime or spiritual visions can come without conscious requests as well, although they generally come after extended spiritual practice and meditation. Following are examples that illustrate the various appearances of intuition, which can be roughly categorized as:

- seemingly un-requested *Eureka!* moments
- consciously requested *Eureka!* moments
- sublime or spiritual visions

THE UN-REQUESTED EUREKA!

Earlier in this book we discussed personality traits and states of mind that naturally encourage intuition. We also touched on the ways that beliefs, which we hold within our unconscious, affect us. These beliefs can color our desires, encourage or discourage intuition and affect the interpretation of any information we receive.

You may wonder how you can have sudden *Eureka!* moments without even asking to receive them. When information seemingly comes to you "out of the blue," then you must have asked a question or made a request at the unconscious level rather than the conscious level.

For instance, this could be a general unstated request for a life of safety and wellbeing and an unconscious desire to live "in flow" with the natural rhythms of life. If you have an unconscious belief that you can successfully take care of yourself, your intuition will support you in creating this reality. A positive attitude opens the doors to receiving intuitions.

In one example, let's say that you quickly assume that everything is good about a person or situation without consciously using the *proving step* for confirmation. As you later reflect upon your quick assumption, you have a sudden negative physical reaction, such as an uncomfortable feeling in the pit of your stomach. This feeling is an *un-requested* intuitive message. It is a valid word of caution that has come to you as the result of that unconscious desire to have a safe life along with your deep belief that you are always meant to be secure.

Intuition can also come to you as a sudden message of danger, although in some cases those signals are not understood until later. For example, let's say you experienced an unexplained urge to leap into your car to leave home earlier than necessary one morning. Later, you hear of a bad accident that occurred on your road to work. Had you left as originally planned, you would have been involved in that accident or at least delayed for some time. You had not consciously requested to avoid an accident that day; however, you maintained that deep ongoing desire to avoid difficulties.

In contrast to this positive state of mind, let us say that you have the unconscious belief that the world is unsafe and you are a victim living under uncomfortable circumstances. In this instance, your unconscious mind assumes that you will be victimized; therefore, your intuition is blocked from bringing you messages of safety in a timely manner. This negative outlook both attracts and proves your negative expectations. With a strong desire, however, you can change this belief. By taking action through a variety of techniques, including psychotherapy and hypnotherapy, you elevate yourself to the higher wisdom of intuition. You can then practice a process, such as the *Eureka! System*, to increase your reception of *un-requested Eureka!* moments.

THE REQUESTED EUREKA!

The *requested Eureka!* appears in answer to a sought-after problem or question. Your request could be either one-time or ongoing. The *Eureka! System* gives you the process for asking for what you want and for receiving answers. The more you practice this intuitive approach to life, the more you will be gifted with messages from your intuition.

For example, many people have definite and ongoing conscious requests for general safety. They welcome true messages of danger. In particular, this can be seen with firefighters, police and those in war zones. Those living in large cities, in unsafe neighborhoods or in unsafe personal relationships also have this conscious desire. They have all acquired, out of experience and necessity, a strong conscious desire for survival. Parents of young children who live with constant and conscious concern for their children's safety also make this request for information about general safety.

An example of an omnipresent conscious request for inspiration comes from Wolfgang Amadeus Mozart. He writes to a friend about how he receives his intuitions:

> *When I am, as it were, completely myself, entirely alone, and of good cheer—say, traveling in a carriage, or walking after a good meal, or during the night when I cannot sleep; it is on such occasions that ideas flow best and most abundantly. Whence and how they come, I know not; nor can I force them.*[2]

Johann Sebastian Bach, when asked to explain the source of his musical scores, answered:

> *The problem is not finding them, it's—when getting up in the morning and getting out of bed—not stepping on them.... I play the notes in order as they are written. It is God who makes the music.*[3]

Through their statements you can see how Mozart and Bach unknowingly initiated their illuminating experiences through their ongoing desire for inspiration. Their desire for guidance was consciously acknowledged, but the fact that this overwhelming desire had set up an open channel to their intuition eluded them. They felt as though they were the blind recipients of *Eureka!* moments rather than initiators of the process. They were so "in flow" with their natural rhythms and desires that they simply lived in the realm of inspiration. Also, it could be said that they were born with both the unconscious belief that they were meant to be creative and the desire to fulfill that belief. They, therefore, experienced the combined strength of both *un-requested* and *requested Eurekas!*

The ways in which intuition is received can appear to contain contradictions: "it is unexpected, but somehow fits; it comes from within, but at the same time from some unnamable other; we produce it, but it also seems to happen to us; we are involved but uninvolved, absorbed but detached."[4]

The Sublime/Spiritual Vision

This third category of intuitions, the *sublime* or *spiritual vision* of pure truth, can come as the result of a conscious or an unconscious request. It involves asking for what you want at a deep level and then receiving an answer that can have universal significance. In the past, this state of receptivity was assumed to be reserved for those immersed in spiritual practices and deep contemplation. Actually, visions and voices have also been bestowed upon unsuspecting innocent souls, such as Joan of Arc. Today, it is a more accepted view that those who are simply open to the experience or willing to expend the effort to reach higher states of receptivity can receive *spiritual visions.*

WHEN AN INTUITION IS NOT AN INTUITION

While, at times, you may struggle with the validity of your own intuitive flashes, there may also be times when you question the truth of another person's claimed intuitive moment. When people tell you that they have relied on their intuition as the basis for their opinions or decisions, should you believe them? Remember, an intuition is defined as an absolute truth.

During your lifetime you may have heard friends, family, coworkers or politicians claim that they have followed their "intuition" or "gut feeling" in making important decisions. These claims may or may not have felt right to you. Possible misstatements by others could have been intentional or unintentional. If intentional, could they have used the word "intuition" as a means for giving credence to their beliefs, opinions or actions? If unintentional, could it be that the path to an actual intuition was blocked or polluted by fear, wishful thinking or some other factor? As you become more comfortable with the intricacies of your intuition, you will find it easier to recognize when an intuition is, or is not, a true intuition.

CAN YOU TRUST YOUR INTUITION?

In many chapters, you find suggestions on how to improve your intuitive abilities. As discussed in Chapter 10, one valuable way to verify whether you have received an authentic intuitive flash is to keep a journal in which you document your experiences. Through the practice of recording an event and then reflecting on it later, you can improve your ability to identify an intuition and, thereby, make better decisions.

Can you ever completely trust your intuition? Yes. Intuition is a natural ability, which is meant to be innately trusted. Yet sometimes it can take a while to get in flow with the rhythms of your inner wisdom. Each time you recognize the truth of an intuition, it adds to your inner confidence and increases your feeling of well being. As you continue to practice ways to become more intuitive, believe and trust in your abilities and accept the remarkable fruits available to you from the intuitive realm, your life can be noticeably changed.

REVIEW QUESTIONS

1. When have you acted on an intuition?

2. What are the three appearances of intuition?

3. What factors do you consider when evaluating another's claim to having received intuitive information?

PART 4

Increasing Your Access to Intuition

*What this power is, I cannot say. All I know is that it exists...
and it becomes available only when you are in that state of
mind in which you know exactly what you want... and are fully
determined not to quit until you get it.*

**—Alexander Graham Bell,
scientist, inventor of the telephone**

Many people ask, "What can I do to increase my intuitive abilities? Are there any tools that you can recommend?" The answer is, "Yes."

It is time now to reveal how you can increase the flow of your intuition through techniques, exercises and practices. These tools are a part of the *Eureka! System*. In particular, you will experience how three practical methods for accessing intuition—meditation, self-hypnosis and dreamwork—can be so profound. The many tools of the *Eureka! System* enable you to begin tapping your intuitive abilities today.

- Chapter 13 – You learn a variety of tools for a variety of situations.
- Chapter 14 – You discover the importance of meditation as well as easy ways to practice it.
- Chapter 15 – You experience what it is like to work with your unconscious mind in self-hypnosis.
- Chapter 16 – You learn how to access your intuition through your dreams.
- Chapter 17 – You see how you can be a more intuitive person and affect your world.

CHAPTER 13
TOOLS FOR INCREASING THE FLOW

"It is always with excitement that I wake up in the morning wondering what my intuition will toss up to me, like gifts from the sea. I work with it and rely on it. It's my partner."

—Jonas Salk, microbiologist who developed the first polio vaccine

In *Step 3* of the *Eureka! System*, tools are used to increase your access to intuition. There are many practices and exercises you can use to either gain immediate intuitive assistance or increase your overall receptivity. You can see which ones fit best for you. Over time you will undoubtedly alter the mix in your toolbox and invent some variations of your own that will be of great value.

Most researchers believe that the first step toward becoming an intuitive person is to make the conscious choice to practice states of mind that invite intuition. These desirable states include a *quiet mind, focused attention, relaxation* and *receptivity to imagery.* Techniques that bring about these states of mind, which are encouraging to intuition, also have the beneficial effect of helping you become less judgmental and more self-aware. These techniques are:

- meditation to quiet the mind and focus attention
- positive affirmations to focus attention
- relaxation exercises to loosen the body and mind
- exercises to encourage imagery
- self-hypnosis to access images and quiet the mind
- dreamwork to increase receptivity

Meditation, self-hypnosis and dreamwork are important tools and larger topics. Therefore, these are covered in full in Chapters 14, 15 and 16.

Focused Attention

Positive Affirmations

It is good to know that you can program your unconscious mind to receive an intuition. This is a simple form of self-hypnosis that involves saying affirmations to yourself as you go through the day. You can say these aloud or repeat them in your head. Because everything you say is taken literally by your unconscious mind, it is wise to become more consciously aware of your self-programming.

You could say to yourself, " Every day in every way, I am more and more intuitive." "I am thankful for all of my intuitions." "I accept and rejoice in my inner wisdom."

You can find more information on how to write affirmations or suggestions under the larger topic of self-hypnosis in Chapter 16.

Relaxation Exercises

Relaxation exercises help you to become calm and more open to intuition.

Yoga

Many researchers recommend yoga for *relaxation* because it has the development of intuition as one of its goals. For years yoga has been used to calm the mind and awaken the inner voice.[1]

In one simple yoga exercise, you can sit or lie comfortably on the floor, become aware of your breathing and talk to your body from the feet upward with phrases such as, "I am relaxing my feet. My feet are relaxing." This assists you in attaining a quieted state of "alert awareness."[2]

BREATHING EXERCISES

With deep breathing, as with any physical exercise, your thoughts are naturally diverted to the physical realm, which reduces mind-chatter. Breathing exercises can also help you access your intuition because:

> Breathing exercises can have a calming and enlivening effect on the nervous system; it is not coincidental that the word inspiration applies both to oxygen intake and creativity.... The brain uses 20 percent of all the oxygen we take in.... [Therefore our breathing] affects not only our tension level but [also] our mental functions.[3]

For a simple daily practice, you can also employ deep abdominal breathing. To do this, sit comfortably with your spine erect. Breathe in through your nose and let your belly, or diaphragm, expand outward. Hold your breath for a few seconds. Then slowly release the air through your nose, letting your abdomen contract. Repeat this a few times. You may experience some dizziness at first, so you will want to take this at your own pace. Over time, and after practicing this a few times a day, this new form of breathing will become as natural to you as the deep and relaxed breathing you experienced when you were born.

Another practice, often recommended before meditating and taught in many yoga classes, is alternate-nostril breathing. For example, breathe in through your left nostril and exhale through your right. Next, breathe in through your right and exhale through your left. Repeat this cycle for five minutes at a sitting if possible.

Edgar Cayce recommends practicing another alternate-nostril breathing procedure before meditation. He suggests that you

> Sit or lie in an easy position, without binding garments... Breathe in through the right nostril three times, and exhale through the mouth. Breathe in three times through the left nostril and exhale through the right.[4]

ALERT RELAXATION TECHNIQUES

Alert relaxation is a technique that is used to relax the body while the mind remains alert to the unconscious world. Three primary medical practitioners have done pioneering research in this area: Edmund Jacobson, Johannes Schultz and Herbert Benson.

In his book, *Progressive Relaxation*, Jacobson discusses the practice of alternately tensing and releasing muscles and doing this in a progressive manner from one end of the body to the other. You can easily abbreviate this method and talk yourself through it in just a few minutes. Most *progressive relaxation* systems today have evolved from Jacobson's early twentieth-century work.[5]

Autogenic training, another relaxation system, was developed by Schultz and based on the research done on hypnosis by Oscar Vogt. In this system, you induce an auto-hypnotic state by repeating sentences such as: "My hand is feeling warmer." "My breathing is becoming calmer."[6] These sentences are devised to control certain physiological responses[7] by bringing attention to specific states, such as heaviness, warmth and breathing, and to areas of the body, such as the limbs, heart, solar plexus and forehead.[8] This method is succinctly explained in Norman Shealy's book, *90 Days to Self-Health*.

The third method of *alert relaxation* was developed by Benson and described in the book, *The Relaxation Response*. It was originally developed for hypertension patients and stems from Benson's research on Transcendental Meditation. There are four elements involved in this system: you establish a quiet environment, find a comfortable sitting position, focus on an object or a one-syllable sound and relax into a passive state. This simple technique is referred to as *clinical meditation*.[9]

INCREASING RECEPTIVITY TO IMAGERY

Even though the word "imagery" appears to refer solely to visual experiences, it involves the formation of mental representations that may be visual, auditory, kinesthetic, gustatory or olfactory. For example, when you are immersed in imagery, within your head you may see a picture, hear a tune, feel something physically, taste or smell something.

Imagery may appear through unconscious or conscious invocation. Images often emerge as the natural result of posing a question to the unconscious mind with or without your conscious awareness of doing so. Imagery can come to you through many inner experiences or altered states such as visions, meditation, self-hypnosis, daydreams, night dreams and lucid dreams.

To develop your *receptivity* to imagery you can practice intentionally invoking images. This is best done after a time spent in meditation or relaxation. By becoming more comfortable with images through your conscious use of them, you can more easily accept the spontaneous images that bubble up in your mind in response to your questions.

Whether images are received spontaneously or induced intentionally, they all need to be interpreted so that you can apply their messages to your life. Premature interpretations, however, are to be avoided for they may foster self-deception and interrupt the flow of further intuitive information. This caution is similar to the one mentioned against "grasping" for intuitive information prematurely. All interpretations are individual and can only be valid in the context of your life. They, also, may or may not be correct.

There are a few things to be aware of when using imagery. First, take care to differentiate your intuitions from desires, fears or fantasies as it is more challenging to correctly interpret purposefully created imagery than those that are involuntarily produced. Next, imagery can also bring you symbols, and these should be interpreted rather than taken literally. At times you may think that you have received cosmic truths, but these could simply be the product of your imagination. And, finally, it is easy to become dependent upon imagery as your primary connection to intuitive wisdom. This can interfere with your recognizing other spontaneous intuitive occurrences.[10]

GUIDED IMAGERY AND SELF-HYPNOSIS

Guided imagery, also referred to as guided visualizations, guided meditation, mental journeys or guided journeys, is a therapeutic technique during which you are led to relax and focus on an image related to an issue that you want to resolve. The therapist, either through an audio recording or a personal appointment, then assists you in working with the imagery. According to the American Holistic Medical Association:

> *Guided imagery and visualization techniques are increasingly used in a variety of conventional and holistic modalities, including autogenic and biofeedback training, hypnotherapy, meditation and psychotherapy.*[11]

For self-hypnosis, you can use guided imagery to induce some change. When you use an audio recording with self-hypnosis, the therapist in the recording helps you move through the imagery. You can also write, record and listen to your own self-hypnosis session with guided imagery that takes you to a special place. There you can ask questions, let yourself receive answers naturally and give gratitude for your experience. (See Chapter 16 for an example that you can practice.)

With both guided imagery and self-hypnosis, you are using your imagination to visualize an improvement or a solution. This invites the participation of your intuitive mind.

IMAGERY EXERCISES

THE LEMON TECHNIQUE

An imagery exercise that can help you improve your abilities is the popular lemon technique. This involves seeing, touching, smelling and finally tasting an illusionary lemon. This exercise, which can be used in self-hypnosis, helps you to become more comfortable with invoking imagery.

To participate in this exercise, read the following paragraph. Then have someone read it to you, or repeat it back to yourself, with your eyes closed.

> *Go ahead, if you will, and let your eyes close. Let yourself begin to relax. Imagine, now, a lemon in front of you in your hand. Notice its shape and texture. What does it feel like? Is it dry or wet? Is it bright or dull? Is there a scent to it or not? Now imagine placing the lemon on a surface, taking a knife and slicing it in two. Now, slice it into quarters. Imagine*

picking up one of the lemon pieces and placing it between your lips. Go ahead and bite down on it. How does it taste? What does it feel like in your mouth and throat? Let yourself notice this for a moment. And when you are finished, go ahead and open your eyes.

What was this exercise like for you? What did you see? What did you feel? What did you taste and smell? As you may have noticed, your nervous system cannot tell the difference between an experience that is real and one that is imagined—it simply reacts to the information you give it.[12]

You have now experienced what it is like to be in trance—the altered state of self-hypnosis and hypnosis. The image of the lemon was deliberately induced, yet the details about it spontaneously appeared in your mind. You were in control, and the images came naturally to you.

The more you practice this exercise, the more comfortable you will become in working with imagery.

THE ROAD AHEAD TECHNIQUE

This exercise is designed to give you "yes" or "no" answers to questions you may have. The answers you receive can give you immediate insight into your situation. Asking your unconscious questions on a frequent basis can increase your ability to elicit images.

For example, you could ask yourself, "Will I get a raise?" and then imagine a path stretching out in front of you. This is the road you see for yourself. Is it sunny or rainy? Is the path rocky and difficult or smooth and easy? Is there a bolder blocking your way?

Another twist on this technique is to see the path ahead of you leading down a hall to a door. In your mind, see this door and practice opening and closing it. Then ask your question once again. Imagine and notice if the door opens for you or is shut in your face. This gives you more information. Remember, this is an exercise designed to increase your familiarity with imagery. Therefore, you are the only one who can correctly interpret your images.

The Crossroads Technique

In another simple *imaging* or visualization procedure, imagine yourself in a situation in which you need to make a decision between two or more alternatives. Assign one of your choices the label "A" and the other choice the label "B." If you have more options, you can repeat this exercise.

Picture yourself walking down a road to a crossroads. There is a sign at the fork in the road that says, "Turn left for choice A. Turn right for choice B. There is no turning back." Which way does your body want to turn? Which road looks the most appealing? If you are unsure, begin down one road and notice what that is like. Then return to the crossroads and test out the other road. Proceed down each of the roads as far as is necessary to gain a sense of what feels or appears right.

Make sure that the images you are receiving are not projections of your fears or desires. Let the images unfold naturally without your controlling them. With continued practice you can become more sensitive to the differences between fears, desires and intuition.

Techniques for Immediate Assistance

A variety of techniques that give you immediate answers to questions can also help you hone your intuitive skills in the long run. These are

- brainstorming alone and with others for problem solving
- *clustering* and *mind mapping* to define questions
- *10-second decisions* to speed decision making
- drawing, dancing and singing to clarify questions
- self-hypnosis to speed solutions

Brainstorming

Brainstorming is a group process for problem solving that invites intuition. Everyone in the group contributes spontaneous ideas and possible solutions to the specific problem at hand. There does not need to be any connection between one idea or opinion and another, although all comments are meant to relate to the stated question. These free-flung comments may, therefore, vary greatly.

The brainstorming system was developed in 1948 by Alex Osborn, author of *Applied Imagination*, and has four rules:

- Present as many ideas as possible.

- Present even the most creative and bizarre ideas.

- Combine, modify and improve on previously presented ideas.

- Do not criticize ideas presented during the session.

The brainstorming session is then followed at least a day later by an evaluation session in which the analytical mind is employed.

CLUSTERING

Clustering, introduced in *Writing the Natural Way* by Gabriele Rico, is a nonlinear writing technique that you can do alone. It is most similar to free association in a writing format. Free association involves making unconstrained associations between thoughts, words and ideas. This activity can access both the analytical and intuitive mind, although it is aimed at tapping into your intuition. Through this system of clustering words on paper, you can organize and expand your thoughts, words and ideas in the development of a question. You may receive more than one intuitive message at a time through the use of this process. Rico writes:

> *To create a cluster you begin with a nucleus word... simply let go and begin to flow with any current of connections that comes into your head.... It has a wisdom of its own.... Should you try to apply logic to what you have clustered, this sense of knowing where you're headed will be destroyed.* [13]

MIND MAPPING

Mind mapping, which is similar to *clustering*, is another writing system that you can use to clarify your questions and encourage the flow of intuitive messages. In this process you consciously lay out multiple subordinate ideas and feelings around the question or problem at hand. In so doing, you may find that some ideas bubble up from your unconscious mind as well. This technique can be found in Tony Buzan's book, *Use Both Sides of Your Brain*, and Joyce Wycoff's book, *Mindmapping*.

10-Second Decisions

Another exercise you can use to improve your skills involves making 10-second decisions in everyday matters. This exercise helps you define problems, raise your overall awareness and increase your sensitivity to the intuitive realm. It is a good practice in which you make immediate predictions on incidental and inconsequential matters, such as guessing the identity of the caller before picking up the phone. Practice this all the time and you will be amazed at your results.[14]

In yet another exercise for quick decision making, allow the same 10 seconds for making a decision around your daily routines, such as what to wear or eat. This is good practice for stretching your comfort level in receiving immediate information from your intuitive mind.[15]

Your Body's Choice

To become better at recognizing intuitive signals, you can practice using your body as an antenna. First, write down a statement or question around an everyday decision you need to make, such as choosing a restaurant for dinner. Next, write down two or more alternative solutions.

Take a few moments to relax and become centered using a breathing exercise. From this neutral space of relaxation, imagine one of your choices, letting the images and feelings appear naturally. Notice how your body reacts. Become neutral once again through your breathing, and imagine another option. Become aware of how that feels in your body as well. Whichever option feels the best is probably your intuitive choice.

REVIEW QUESTIONS

1. What desirable states of mind invite intuition?

2. What positive affirmation might be appropriate for you at this time?

3. Practice one of the breathing techniques for 3 to 5 minutes. Note how you feel before you begin and then after you finish.

4. Practice the lemon technique for yourself. Notice what you experience.

5. Practice the 10-second decisions exercises several times over the next few days. Notice what you experience.

CHAPTER 14
MEDITATION: A KEY TOOL

By the power of concentration and meditation you can direct the inexhaustible power of your mind to accomplish what you desire and to guard every door against failure.

—Paramahansa Yogananda, author of *Autobiography of a Yogi*

Meditation acts as the solid foundation for any intuitive work. A regular meditation practice is considered to be necessary because it quiets the conscious mind.[1]

Throughout the ages mystics have recommended that we take up a meditation practice to quiet mind-chatter and increase self-awareness. There are many styles of meditation in Eastern and Western traditions. Although they each achieve different states of consciousness, all are designed to shift the focus from the outward experience of the analytical mind to the inward experience of the unconscious, or intuitive, mind.

The method of meditation is not as important as the regular practice of it. Meditation is practiced to let go of old beliefs and agendas so that you can create a space for new ideas and intuitions. Through a stance of non-judgmental observation and detached awareness you can acknowledge thoughts and feelings that bubble up during meditation without attempting to judge or change them.

Meditation enables you to become more open and focused in the moment. This allows you to be more responsive to the intuitive messages that you see, hear, feel and know. With practice, you naturally become more self-aware and compassionate toward yourself and others.[2]

Transcendental Meditation— A Meditation Technique

Transcendental Meditation, or TM, was developed by Maharishi Mahesh Yogi in the late 1950s to appeal to a Western audience.[3] It is a simple method that relaxes the mind; and as your mind quiets and you are able to focus, the doors are opened to the many facets of your intuition.

Neither a religion or a philosophy, nor a way of life, Transcendental Meditation is a natural technique for reducing stress and expanding conscious awareness.
—Bloomfield, Cain, and Jaffe, authors on transcendental meditation

---

TM is widely available and its results are scientifically document- ed. To give you a general idea about how it works, an instructor teaches you the method, gives you an individual mantra (a word or phrase) and then is available to give you feedback to ensure your success. TM takes only twenty minutes in the morning and twenty minutes in the evening to practice. By repeating the word, or mantra, your mind is brought back from wandering thoughts and is cleared of daily mind- chatter. This relaxing and clearing of the mind has the effect of refresh- ing the body just as a nap would do.

Because TM is so effective, other systems are based upon it, such as that developed by Herbert Benson, M.D., and explained in the book, *The Relaxation Response*. Benson did clinical research with TM and found that repeating the word "one" issued similar results to using a personal mantra. In my personal experience, TM helped me achieve success through clearing and focusing my mind:

After learning TM in high school, I went from being a "C" student to an honors student almost overnight. With a clearer mind and a more relaxed body, the inspiration for poetry easily flowed through me. As a result I received awards for my work.

To write well you have to access your creative nature—your intuition. Meditation assists you in accessing inspiration and inner truth. John Keats, the inspired British poet, reflected on the importance of inspiration: "If poetry comes not as naturally as the leaves to a tree it had better not come at all."[4] And the Scottish writer Thomas Carlyle spoke on the importance of being able to access this sense of inner knowing. He stated that, "Healthy understanding... is not... logical [or] argumentative, but [instead] intuitive; for the end of understanding is not to prove and find reasons, but to know and believe."[5]

TM took off in the 1970s after it was endorsed by the Beatles and New York Jets quarterback Joe Namath.
—**Thomas Tweed and Stephen Prothero, authors**

A SIMPLE MEDITATION TECHNIQUE

Understanding how to meditate is important, and practice makes it meaningful. If you don't yet have a preferred technique, the following is a simple meditation you can begin using today. You can practice this for ten or twenty minutes at a sitting. Note what you discover.

1. Begin by finding a quiet place where there will be no distractions or interruptions. Later, after you have practiced for a while, you will discover that you are able to meditate in almost any environment.

2. Sit comfortably in a chair. Let your spine be straight, let your head follow your spine, place your feet flat on the floor and let your hands rest comfortably in your lap with your palms facing upwards. Posture is important.

3. Let your eyes hold a soft gaze on the floor somewhat in front of you. If you prefer, you may close your eyes.

4. Now, begin counting your breathing. This is your focus. Take in a full deep breath through your nose, and as you let it out through your nose say "ten" to yourself. Now, take in another deep breath and as you let that out say "nine" to yourself. Continue counting down in this way until you reach one. Then

begin again with ten and continue the cycle from ten to one for the full 10 or 20 minutes.

5. Relax into this experience. Allow yourself to be present and open to your intuition. Whenever you find yourself drifting, just notice that and take yourself back to your breathing and counting. If you become physically or emotionally uncomfortable, notice that as well and return to your breathing.

6. When you sense that your chosen time has elapsed, you may gently glance at the clock. This is preferable to using an alarm. As you continue to practice meditation, your intuition will let you know when your time has elapsed.

7. When you have completed your meditation, fully open your eyes and notice how you feel.

Breaking Through Old Beliefs

All meditation techniques begin to break down the old beliefs and patterns that no longer serve you and interfere with your self-awareness. As you continue with any one of these practices, you find that your mind-chatter dissipates allowing you to become more aware of yourself and your environment. As you become more present, you increase your receptivity to intuition.

Perhaps you will begin to notice subtle shifts in your perspectives—you may begin to see yourself and others differently. As you have more space for your own thoughts, feelings and intuitions, you may become more compassionate with yourself. Simply notice and enjoy where this takes you.

Review Questions

1. Why is meditation practice so foundational in intuitive work?

2. Practice the simple meditation technique a few times. What do you notice?

3. How can meditation help you break through old inhibiting beliefs?

CHAPTER 15

SELF-HYPNOSIS: A PROVEN TOOL

*When I worked on the polio vaccine, I had a theory.
I guided each [experiment] by imagining myself in the
phenomenon in which I was interested. The intuitive realm...
the realm of the imagination guides my thinking.*

**—Jonas Salk, microbiologist who developed
the first polio vaccine**

Self-hypnosis has been proven to be a valid tool for accessing intuitive states of mind and intuitive insights.[1] It facilitates your access to unconscious processes,[2] You can use self-hypnosis to quiet your mind, thereby increasing your receptivity to intuition. You can also use it to evoke imagery[3] for answers to questions you may have.

COMPARING SELF-HYPNOSIS AND MEDITATION

Meditation and self-hypnosis both relax the analytical mind, decrease mind-chatter and draw attention inward to the unconscious mind where you can break down any interfering structures. This makes you more open and available to intuition.

The purpose of meditation, however, differs from that of self-hypnosis. In meditation, you are less active, and the overall objective is to quiet the mind. Once the mind is quieted, various styles of meditation focus on either emptying the mind, expanding awareness, developing concentration, focusing attention or helping you to become centered.

By contrast, in self-hypnosis, you are looking for an answer to a problem or a question or an improvement in a situation. After you relax your conscious mind, you proceed inward with the intention of giving the unconscious mind suggestions, "to increase motivation or alter behavior patterns."[4] These commanding suggestions are typical of the more traditional, or directive, style of self-hypnosis. They often take the form of repetitive positive affirmations or visualizations.

In the more transpersonal, or permissive, forms of self-hypnosis, however, you also watch and listen to the imagery that appears before you in response to the hypnotic suggestions. Through interacting with imagery you experience a natural evolution that gives you additional information about yourself or your situation. This unfolding of the image either leads you to your goals or shows you additional steps that you can take to reach them. In this way you are taking a more active role in working with your unconscious material and the wisdom issued from your intuitive mind.

A Brief History of Hypnosis

For thousands of years shamans—wise medicine men and women of indigenous tribes—have used trance-like states to access intuition for wisdom and healing. Drumming, dancing, singing, medicinal plants and rigorous ordeals assist shamans and others in entering altered states of consciousness. By altering their awareness they are better able to access intuition and affect change. Such shamans were the first hypnotists.

Since the late 1700s, hypnosis has been used by medical doctors, psychotherapists and others to improve people's health and well being.[5] According to a feature article in the *Wall Street Journal*, "Hypnosis, often misunderstood and almost always controversial, is increasingly being employed in mainstream medicine."[6] David Spiegel, a Stanford University psychologist, stated in the article that:

> *Hypnosis may sound like magic, but we are now producing evidence showing it can be significantly therapeutic. We know it works but we don't know how, though there is some science beginning to figure that out, too.[7]*

Some Facts About Hypnosis

A general understanding of hypnosis can help you feel more comfortable and confident when utilizing the self-hypnosis process outlined in this chapter. Hypnosis is a state of consciousness that you go in and out of naturally all the time. It is similar to "zoning out" while watching television or becoming absorbed in a novel. It is a twilight state similar to daydreaming.

To define it further, hypnosis is an altered state in which you become relaxed, your conscious mind-chatter is quieted, your attention is focused inwardly and you are more open to suggestions. Because the hypnotic state is self-generated, all hypnosis is actually self-hypnosis. In other words, you cannot be put into a trance state without your consent, and the suggestions you are given in hypnosis can be either accepted or rejected by you at will.

Hypnosis uses guided imagery and invites spontaneously produced additional images. During hypnosis you are more able to access your imagination, emotions, memories and deeper aspects of yourself. Your attention is free to examine, deprogram and reprogram thoughts, feelings, and behaviors that no longer serve you. By bypassing the conscious mind, you can more easily access your intuition.[8]

During a session you are aware of your surroundings, while at the same time you can concentrate on your internal imagery. Returning from a trance state is as natural as returning from a dream. And after you return, you can generally remember what took place during the hypnosis session and can reflect upon it. Essentially, everyone can be hypnotized—success depends on motivation and trust.

We are all pretty expert in unconsciously using self-hypnosis.
—David Cheek, M.D., author on hypnosis

DEFINING SELF-HYPNOSIS

Self-hypnosis, also called auto-hypnosis, is a self-created state of relaxation in which you are more open to your intuition. It differs from hypnosis in that you access the hypnotic state without the personalized guidance of a hypnotist or hypnotherapist.

In self-hypnosis, just as in hypnosis, you reduce your orientation to external reality[9] while increasing your receptivity to internal experiences.[10] To go into trance you can read a script that you composed or use one written by someone else. You can also listen to an audio recorded either by you or another. Hypnotic inductions are applied at the beginning of all hypnosis and self-hypnosis sessions to take you into your unconscious mind.

The induction portion of any script includes instructions for relaxation.[11] It can also include breathing exercises and guided imagery. The meaning you assign to the images, feelings, thoughts and altered body perceptions that arise during this process determine whether you feel you have succeeded in accessing your intuition.[12]

Graham Wallas, author of the four stages of thought, recommends self-hypnosis during his incubation stage. This quiets the mind and brings about a state of relaxation, which is known to be necessary for accessing intuition.[13] Milton Fisher, intuition researcher, also recommends self-hypnosis because, "Hypnosis relaxes the subject so deeply that his conscious [mind] is placed in a recessive role and the intuitive [mind] becomes dominant."[14] This drops conscious resistance and calms the fears that emanate from mental chatter. The intuitive mind is then given a voice to speak. With self-hypnosis giving you such important access to your intuitive mind, Agor recommends self-hypnosis for business executives.[15]

Hypnotherapy... is one of several relaxation methods for treating chronic pain that has been approved by an independent panel convened by the National Institutes of Health.
—The Mayo Clinic

DEFINING HYPNOTHERAPY

To give you a simple definition, hypnotherapy uses hypnosis, as defined above, for therapeutic purposes. So when a therapist places a subject in hypnosis, it is called hypnotherapy. In 1955, the British Medical Association approved hypnotherapy as a valid medical treatment. Three years later, in 1958, it was approved by the American Medical Association. In general, hypnotherapists work with functional individuals who want to change behaviors and improve their quality of life. Psychologists and psychiatrists with hypnotherapy training may also choose to work with individuals who have mental disorders.

Hypnotherapy has been used for a wide variety of conditions and is primarily known for its success with stress, fear, pain, weight issues and negative or unwanted behaviors. Along with insight-oriented psychotherapy, hypnotherapy is used to assist you in letting go of images that were misconstrued in the past and buried in your memory banks in the form of distorted memories.[16]

TRANSPERSONAL HYPNOTHERAPY DEFINED

There are various forms of hypnotherapy, and these primarily follow the four "schools" of psychology: (1) psychoanalytic, (2) behavioral, (3) humanistic and (4) transpersonal. The more traditional forms of hypnotherapy focus on the first two waves of psychology. Hypnoanalysis, like psychoanalysis, examines root causes of problems. Behavior modification, like behavioral psychology, aims at achieving a specific change in behavior. Transpersonal hypnotherapy utilizes these first two techniques while emphasizing the last two. Self-actualization (or the integration of body, mind and emotions, which is the goal of humanistic psychology) and self-transcendence (or the realization of spiritual potential, which is the focus of transpersonal psychology) are the aims of transpersonal hypnotherapy.[17]

In transpersonal hypnotherapy, as in transpersonal psychology, there is a blending of Eastern and Western views of human nature. It assumes that there is more to you than merely your personality. The goal here is to transcend the restrictions of your personality (or ego), heighten your awareness and access the wisdom of your full soul, which is available to you through your intuition. This brings you a greater sense of inner directedness and personal freedom that you can enjoy in your daily life.

On a personal note, since co-developing the system of transpersonal hypnotherapy in the late 1980s, I have been witness to its effectiveness, both in my private practice and in the practices of my graduates. This approach to hypnotherapy invites a personal relationship with your intuition—your access to realms of universal truth and absolute knowledge. The transpersonal approach is used in the self-hypnosis script below to access your inner wisdom.

DESIGNING YOUR SELF-HYPNOSIS SESSION

Before entering a self-hypnosis session, you want to consciously ask for what you want. Next, clarify your desires more fully. You will find that you also clarify them more fully when you are in trance. What do you want to be, do or have? During the session you can expect some form of an answer, or a solution, to arise from your intuition.

DESIGNING QUESTIONS AND STATEMENTS

To design questions for your unconscious mind (#7 and #8 below), consider what you would like to know about yourself or a particular situation. First, write simple questions using the words "what" or "how" to engage your intuitive mind. Words such as "why" engage your analytical mind instead.

Some examples of questions around your intuition could be, "What is blocking me from receiving my intuition?" Next you could ask, "How can I remove these blockages?" In session, allow time for the imagery from your intuition to show you answers in the forms of visions, words and feelings. In this way you can gain insights about yourself and move ahead.

Some examples of questions around other issues could be, "What is the benefit for my staying in this relationship?" "How can I do better at work?" "How can I reach my desired weight?"

If you want a "yes" or "no" answer to a question, you can make a statement that describes two possible scenarios surrounding your situation. Your unconscious mind will then bring forth imagery—visions, words and feelings. Your reaction to the imagery will give you the answer. For example, if you are trying to decide between two jobs, you can make the statement, "I accept the job with Company X." Notice what images arise. Next state, "I stay with my current job," and notice what images arise from that assertion. This process gives you your answers.

DESIGNING HYPNOTIC SUGGESTIONS

While in self-hypnosis, you give yourself suggestions (#9 and #10 below) that carry your desires from your unconscious mind into your consciousness. These suggestions have to do with what you want to be, what you want to do or what you want to have.

Some examples of well-written suggestions for intuition are: "I am open and receptive to my intuition." "I do that which is in my highest good and for the highest good of all life." "I appreciate my intuition and all that it brings me."

Some examples of other possible suggestions are, "I do my part to enjoy all of my relationships." "I listen to feedback and communicate clearly at work." "I eat those foods that truly nourish me."

When you are giving yourself suggestions, notice how you respond to the imagery. Place yourself within an image and experience the desired results from your suggestions. For example, feel what it is like, and notice what you say to yourself, when you are open and receptive to your intuition.

Here are some guidelines for designing effective suggestions:

- Write simple suggestions (positive affirmations).
- Use direct and clear language.
- Use the present tense, not future tense.
- Use positive wording and avoid the word "try."
- Use imagery to elicit desired sensations, feelings and responses.

OUTLINE OF A SELF-HYPNOSIS SESSION

The following is an outline of a self-hypnosis session that you can administer for yourself. You can customize it for particular questions and situations.

1. Make yourself comfortable, either sitting or lying down.

2. Focus on your breathing.

3. Instruct yourself to go deeper into a relaxed state.

4. Note the duration and purpose of your session. (Tell yourself how many minutes you will be in trance, what you want to ac-

complish, and that you will return refreshed, relaxed and alert at the conclusion.)

5. Count yourself down from 10 to 1. (Tell yourself you will be going down a set of steps, going further into trance with each number.)

6. Mentally transport yourself to a special place of comfort, relaxation and safety. Fully immerse yourself in it.

7. Ask yourself a question or make a statement. Ask yourself a follow-up question or make a second statement.

8. Notice how the imagery of your unconscious mind responds.

9. Give yourself suggestions to be, do or have what you want.

10. Again, notice how the imagery of your unconscious mind responds.

11. Give yourself the suggestion to return refreshed, able to remember whatever is important for you to remember and able to return to this trance-like state more easily every time.

The 10-Minute Self-Hypnosis Script for Accessing Intuition

The following self-hypnosis script is designed to help you increase access to your intuition. Because, in this script, you are not correcting a problem other than a possible lack of access, there is little deprogramming involved within it. Your intuitive mind, in its purity, holds great wisdom. Therefore, this script is primarily designed to engage the wisdom of your intuition through your unconscious mind.

You can read it in third person, as it is written below, by using phrases such as: "You can let your eyes close now." In this way you are giving yourself suggestions, as a hypnotherapist would do. Or, you can switch to first person and state: "I am now letting my eyes close." How you state this is solely a matter of personal preference.

Simply read, record and play it back to yourself, or read it a few times, become comfortable with it and repeat it to yourself in your mind while you are in trance. You can use this script every day if you like, for the more you repeat the process, the easier it becomes. To begin,

Make yourself comfortable now, Go ahead and let your eyes close. Begin focusing your attention on your breathing, in and out... in and out. There is nothing to do and nowhere to go. Simply become aware of your breathing in and out.... And with every breath you begin to go deeper, deeper into a healing state of peace and relaxation, letting your attention become absorbed in your breathing.

Now, let yourself know that you will remain in this state for the next seven minutes. You will then return from this hypnotic state feeling refreshed, relaxed and better than before.

During this session you will be asking questions of your intuitive mind and giving yourself positive self-suggestions about how you would like to be, what you would like to do and what you would like to have. Let your mind begin to open itself to the suggestions. Ask your unconscious to accept only those suggestions that are in your highest good and for the highest good of all life.

In a moment you will count down from ten to one and go deeper into trance, using the metaphor of going down ten safe, secure steps. Counting down now, with each number going deeper into trance....

Ten, starting down the steps and beginning to go deeper.

Nine, continuing down the steps.

Eight, with every step going deeper.

Seven, feeling yourself going deeper, deeper than before.

Six, becoming more and more open to your intuition.

Five, going deeper still, twice as deep as before.

Four, deeper and deeper.

Three, becoming more comfortable, more relaxed and wondering what it might be like for your unconscious mind to open up to suggestions that are in your highest good.

Two, deeper still... and, one, feeling what deeper really feels like.

Now, if you will, take a moment and say to yourself, "I am now in a deep, more relaxed state of trance."

And, now, mentally transport yourself to a place of comfort, relaxation and safety. This could be a place in your inner world, or a place in your outer world where you've been before. It really doesn't matter. What matters is that you feel comfortable and relaxed and open to your intuition here.

Immerse yourself in this place now. Notice the sights, sounds, smells and feelings. Notice how comfortable it is to be in a place where you can open up to your intuition.

Now present your question to your unconscious mind.

(Insert questions or statements here.)

Let your intuition enter the scene to answer. It may come to you in a variety of forms: a symbol, a color or an image of you or something else. Notice what it looks like and feels like. As you become aware of it, notice that it has information for you. Let yourself receive it. Notice how you react.

(Allow a minute of quiet time to notice what your intuition brings to you.)

And, now, give yourself suggestions about what you would like to be, do or have.

(Insert suggestions here.)

See, sense and feel what it is like to be, or do or have what you want. Let your intuition show you these images.

(Allow a minute of quiet time to notice what your intuition brings to you.)

Now in a moment you will count yourself back from one to three, becoming more alert and aware with every number, knowing that your intuitive mind is now working with you for your highest good. You have planted the seed, and it is time to let it grow. It is time to let it manifest in your life, in its own perfect timing and in its own perfect way.

And, now, as you begin to become more alert, bring your intuitive insights back with you. Notice what it is like to be in touch with your inner wisdom.

Now, counting back, one... two... and three. Letting your eyes open, feeling refreshed and better than before, able to remember everything you desire to remember, whenever you desire to do so, and able to return to this state more easily and effortlessly every time.

As soon as you return from this state, take a few moments to write in your journal your experiences and *Eureka!* moments. This validates what you have learned about yourself. It also lets your intuition know that you want to communicate with it more fully.

RESULTS ACHIEVED THROUGH SELF-HYPNOSIS AND HYPNOTHERAPY

The more you practice self-hypnosis, the greater your results will be. This process gives you a quick tool for making both small and large decisions in partnership with your intuitive mind. It also can be a tool for healing yourself. For example,

As a freshman in college, I began using self-hypnosis, hypnotherapy and journaling to improve my health. Two years previous, I had been in a car accident and continued to suffer from the pain of whiplash-type injuries. Through working directly with my intuition, I was able to achieve amazing results with my body—the pain was eliminated for good.

REVIEW QUESTIONS

1. How does self-hypnosis differ from meditation?

2. Design a self-hypnosis session for yourself.

3. Record and then listen to the 10-Minute Self-Hypnosis Script. What was your experience?

CHAPTER 16

DREAMWORK: A POWERFUL TOOL

We must at least agree that the things seen by us in sleep are... like painted images, and cannot have been formed save in the likeness of what is real and true.

—René Descartes, philosopher and scientist

The imagery we receive through dreaming, either through parts of a dream or from the dream as a whole, can bring us important messages. Allowing time for preparation and incubation before entering sleep is key. In their book, *Dreamworking*, Stanley Krippner and Joseph Dillard state that,

> *Preparation and incubation are necessary if illumination and inspiration are to occur in dreams.... One can hardly expect solutions to problems to spring full blown from one's dreams like children from the head of Zeus.[1]*

Dreams, as well as lucid dreams—those times during which you maintain conscious awareness in the dream state[2]—provide you with an important channel of receptivity to intuitive insights. Images can be direct intuitive truths, or truths that are metaphorical. In lucid dreams you can move into the dream and voluntarily evoke additional images.[3]

DREAM INTERPRETATION

Interpreting the spontaneous images you receive visually, auditorily and kinesthetically is a valuable practice because it lets your intuition know that you are listening. Your dreams can give you all the information you need, even though at times you may not want to hear the message. By remaining as non-judgmental as possible, you can delve more fully into their meanings. [4]

According to Carl Jung, as with any imagery, "No dream symbol can be separated from the individual who dreams it; there is no definite or straightforward interpretation of any dream."[5] So let your intuition lead you through your dreams and lucid dreams as well as through your interpretation of them. And take care not to willfully manipulate lucid dreams.[6]

Sharing dreams with a friend or a dream group gives you a format for reflecting upon the images you have received. When sharing, remember that the interpretations are ultimately yours.

TOOLS FOR SLEEP, DREAMING AND JOURNALING

You can experiment to find out whether your dreams are more memorable after nap time or after a night's sleep. Once you become comfortable with the process in one area, you can transfer your skills to the other. Before going to sleep and upon awakening, you can apply many practical tools for increasing your ability to remember and understand dreams.

PRE-SLEEP RITUALS

Before you go to bed, let your unconscious know that you are preparing for dreams:

- Make your sleeping area comfortable and pleasant. This may mean upgrading your bedding so that your physical body can relax and you can feel good about yourself while going to sleep. You can place fresh or silk flowers in the room to add color and life. Do anything that lets you know that you are appreciating you.

- Take a warm bath or shower before bed so that your body feels fresh, clean and relaxed for your dream adventure. Washing away the day allows you to begin anew at night.

- Play some soothing music for a few minutes, perhaps while you are in the bath. This allows you to shift out of the day and into a place where you are truly being good to yourself.

- Spray the room with an appealing scent before sleep. This gives your mind the signal that you are now preparing for an important journey.

- Meditate before sleep, even if it is for only a few minutes. You can do this while you are in the tub or settling into bed before you go to sleep. This cleanses your mind and opens you to the wisdom of your spirit.

- Place a pencil and your dream journal next to your bed. Your journal should be easy to open, such as a spiral notebook, because you may be writing in bed.

PRE-SLEEP PROGRAMMING

Once you are in bed, you can say the following to yourself in the present tense. You want to speak to yourself in the present tense because that is the only time frame within which your mind knows how to create:

- I am entering a deep, sound sleep.
- During my sleep I have dreams that bring me intuitive wisdom.
- These dreams have meaning only for me. I honor them.
- Upon awakening I remember my dreams and write them down.
- I allow enough time in my daily schedule to relax into this process.
- I give thanks for my intuition.
- I commence sleeping and dreaming now.

ACTIVITIES UPON AWAKENING

When you awaken, you are still in contact with your dream:

- Allow a half-hour or more to communicate with your dreams.
- Awaken naturally or with a soothing alarm.
- Keep your silence. Do not talk with anyone during this time.
- Remain in a quiet state of reverie wherein you have access to your unconscious mind.

- Slowly turn over in bed and position yourself to write. Or get up slowly and make your way to a comfortable chair for writing.

- Remain relaxed and in that place of non-judgment that is afforded you during sleep.

- Allow the dream to come forward and unfold for you now.

- Journal your dreams.

- If a dream doesn't come forward, say, "Thank you, unconscious mind, for engaging in this process. I ask that I become better at this with every dawning day."

DREAM JOURNALING

When you are writing in your journal, you are connecting with your dreams:

- Write down your dreams in the present tense and from the "I" perspective. For example, you could write, "I am in the dream. I see myself sitting by the side of the road."

- Write each significant thought on a new line to make it easier to read later.

- Include all the specifics, such as what you saw, heard, and felt emotionally and physically.

- Give each dream a number and title. For example, "Dream #1: Sitting by the Side of the Road."

- Then go back and read the first dream to yourself.

- Become each part of your dream. (See the Gestalt technique below.)

GESTALT DREAM INTERPRETATION

Numerous methods for interpreting dreams exist. Gestalt dream interpretation, developed by Gestalt therapy founder Fritz Perls (1893-1970), addresses all aspects of the dream experience so that you can broaden your self-awareness. This is a simple yet powerful method for increasing self-knowledge around a particular issue.

Gestalt therapy was developed to help you integrate the different perspectives—or opinions—you have about yourself into a whole and complete understanding of who you are. Through increasing your self-awareness around what you are doing and why you are doing it, you can gain insights as to the ways in which you can change.[7]

In Gestalt dreamwork, the dreamer is instructed to identify with every image in the dream, assuming that everything in the dream represents a disowned or projected aspect of the self.[8]

Through this technique you can increase your self awareness, thereby making more inner space available for your intuition.

AN EXAMPLE OF A DREAM

Dreamwork can be simple and fun. You can learn how to interpret your dreams through example, practice and connecting with your intuition. For the sake of learning through an example, let's interpret one of my dreams:

I see a long hallway in front of me. I hear a voice and see a light coming from the doorway at the end of the hall. I feel cold and scared at first, but then I feel this deep sense of calm. As I make my way to the door, I feel the warm, smooth floor beneath my feet. It is smoother than I have ever felt before. It almost seems like satin. In fact, the air on my skin feels smooth, too, and there is a scent of burnt vanilla in the air. I can almost taste it.

AN EXAMPLE OF DREAM INTERPRETATION

Following is an example of using the Gestalt method of dream interpretation in which you become each part of the dream to gain varying points of view on your situation. Next, you become the dream as a whole to gain a general overall perspective. Throughout this experience, you move through the dream in the present tense. This is a valuable exercise in self-discovery—it can open the channels of your intuition.

As you follow along with my interpretations below, take a moment to pause with each number and make an interpretation for yourself.

Become each aspect of the dream and then become the dream as a whole. This will give you good practice.

1. I am the hallway. I feel lonely but I am not alone. I am not sure what is ahead of me, but it feels soothing.

2. I am the door. I open and close according to what is in front of me. If it feels cool, I close down and keep the warmth inside of me. If it warms up, I am willing to open up as well.

3. I am the floor. People abuse me at times, though most of the time they don't even know I am here. I don't like being treated that way. Sometimes I feel as though I should just give up. But then I remember I have a purpose. If other people don't like me, at least I can like myself. As I say that, I feel a warmth come over me. It is comforting. Then, when I feel people walking on me, I feel their warmth, too. As their feet touch my back, it feels good. I don't feel abused and walked on any more. I actually feel at one with the people. I now know that if I open up to myself, feel more and love myself more, that others will love me, too. We will then enjoy the journey together as one.

4. I am the air. I am the blessing that comes from union with all that is. This is the natural state of things. I am simply a part of everything. It is good.

5. I am the scent in the air. When all is one, there is a synchronistic effect that cannot be had in any other way. It is when all things work together that I am emitted into the air. It feels good to be the result of such good things. I can actually be tasted by those in the physical realm when I am present in their reality. Goodness abounds when we are one.

6. I am the person walking down the hall. At first I am scared, but then I let go of my fear, and the negativity around me begins to dissolve. I wonder if this new sense of well being will work for me at the office. All thoughts come together in a calm excitement as I make my way to the light and the voice behind the door. I know that the answers are there for me. I just have to look.

7. Now, I am the dream as a whole. I make my way through the

fear and move ahead to the intuitive wisdom within me. This feels good. All the answers I need are within reach.

How was it for you to go through each aspect of the dream? With practice you can fully imagine yourself as each part of your own dreams. Interpreting them can become an enriching part of your day.

ANSWERS UPON AWAKENING

Beyond this, if you continuously ask yourself questions in earnest throughout the day and upon going to bed at night, you are often given the answers not only through the images in your dreams, but also through the messages that are flashed to you immediately upon awakening. These flashed answers may come through a simple sense of knowing or words you hear in your head. Here is one illustration of that:

I often awaken singing songs—sometimes with the exact words and sometimes with altered phrases to relay particular meanings. This habit seems odd to me since I rarely listen to the radio and am often surprised that I even know the song. This is one way, however, that my intuition happens to speak to me. For example,

While writing this book I had a challenging day during which I asked myself the question, "How will I get all of this work done?" "How can I get through this?" "Will I have a life ever again?" The next morning I awoke singing these words, "Ooh, ooh, child, things are going to get easier. Ooh, ooh, child, things will get brighter. Some day, you'll pull it together and you'll get it all done. Some day, things will get lighter." Having received this intuition, I was then able to relax and continue.

The assistance you receive from your intuition can be this simple and joyful. You will find that it speaks to you in many curious ways.

REVIEW QUESTIONS

1. Practice the pre-sleep rituals, pre-sleep programming and activities upon awakening. What do you experience with this process?

2. Record a dream in your dream journal.

3. Use the Gestalt dream interpretation method to interpret your dream. What do you discover about yourself?

CHAPTER 17
PULLING IT
ALL TOGETHER

*Knowing others is intelligence; knowing yourself
is true wisdom. Mastering others is strength;
mastering yourself is true power.*

**—Lao-Tsu, founder of Taoism,
author of *Tao Te Ching***

In this book we have covered centuries of thought and research
on intuition. Now we will review a few of the more pertinent
ideas. We have talked about:

- 2,500 years of understanding and defining intuition
- the ways in which you receive intuition
- personality traits that encourage intuition
- intuition in the workplace
- states and traits that inhibit intuition
- accessing intuition using the *Eureka! System*
- techniques for increasing intuition
- tools of meditation, self-hypnosis and dreamwork

*Intuition is the act or faculty of knowing immediately,
directly and holistically without rational processes
and without being aware of how we know. It is also
the channel through which we access realms of universal
truth, absolute knowledge and ultimate reality.*

WAYS YOU RECEIVE INTUITIVE INFORMATION

By understanding the various ways in which you receive intuition, you can become more aware of the intuitive insights you might otherwise dismiss or overlook. You may have noticed that you are naturally more inclined to receive intuition through one mode more frequently than others. At various times intuitions might appear in a combination of ways:

- mental images, symbols and words
- emotional feelings
- physical feelings
- spiritual knowledge
- environmental situations

Unexpected and un-requested flashes can come to you at any time and may be unrecognized for a while. Requested flashes may appear at any time following your conscious search for an answer to a question or problem. Sublime or spiritual revelations may be awaiting your heartfelt search for inspiration.

HOW TO ENCOURAGE YOUR INTUITION

To encourage success in the intuitive process you can:

- attain positive states of mind
- become more focused
- practice using tools that you enjoy
- create pleasant physical surroundings
- have loving interactions that foster your self-esteem
- practice your chosen processes
- maintain belief, faith and trust in your intuition

Depending upon your personal characteristics, you may prefer using some of the tools more than others. At times, certain techniques will be more applicable to your situation or needs, and therefore you are likely to implement those with greater success.

To succeed at increasing and applying your intuition, you will want to practice as much as possible. Thomas Edison, who failed in over 10,000 initial attempts to develop the light bulb, felt that he was preparing himself for the next revelation with every trial.[1] He did not fail, for he was willing to take a risk with each creative action. His every result created an opening for the next discovery.[2] Edison's belief and faith in the possibilities and his trust in his intuition kept him moving ahead.

INHIBITORS TO AVOID

It is important to be aware of the personality traits and states of mind that inhibit intuition so that you can you can strive to avoid them. The number one blockage is fear in its many forms. Conscious or unconscious fear is a multifaceted inhibitor that can keep you from beginning the intuitive process, stop you from relaxing fully, block you from proceeding through the steps and prevent you from receiving intuitive knowledge. Fear can also distort your interpretations and interrupt your implementation of the results.

Stress can be a major component in blocking your intuitive wisdom. Intrusive thoughts, unsettling emotions or someone else's influence can also muddy or distort your vision. An unrealistic self-image, and any form of negativity, can also interfere with your awareness of intuitive signals and pollute your interpretations. Finally, not only negative thinking, but also wishful thinking, can contaminate your acknowledgment and interpretation of any intuitive insight.

An absolute can only be given in an intuition,
while all the rest has to do with analysis.
—Henri Bergson, philosopher,
Nobel Prize winner in literature

How to Achieve Your Goals with the *Eureka!* System

The seven step *Eureka! System* offers you a comprehensive, yet fluid and practical, approach to developing your intuitive faculty. It is designed to make your life easier and more enjoyable because you are meant to live in flow with the creative nature of your intuition.

To become more intuitive you can simply follow the *ACT* and *LEAP* formula for success:

Step 1: *Ask* for what you want: "I want to be intuitive."

Step 2: *Clarify* this by stating your desire more exactly. "I want to be more intuitive at work... at home...."

Step 3: Use your *Tools.*

- Experiment with the various techniques.
- Get in the habit of saying positive affirmations to yourself.
- Start meditating for a few minutes every day.
- Record the self-hypnosis script from this book and play it back to yourself a few times a week.
- Keep a dream journal.

Step 4: *Let go* of thinking about your desires. Simply enjoy your meditations, take long walks, find reasons to appreciate yourself and genuinely engage in life.

Step 5: *Eureka!* Appreciate the moments you feel aware and in flow. Feel what it is like to access your intuition.

Step 6: *Act* upon your *Eureka!* moments. Recognize them as being authentic.

Step 7: Look for *Proof* in your actions. Notice the ideas that were off in their accuracy yet proved to be valuable teaching tools. Appreciate the authentic flashes, for they can make a significant difference in your life.

You Can Be the Intuitive Person

Just as you are born with five senses, so are you born with intuition. The potential to master this faculty is within you—it simply takes practice.

You can start exercising your intuition by experimenting with some tools to discover those that you enjoy. Then, pick a form of meditation that appeals to you and begin your practice. This gives you a solid basis upon which to build your intuitive abilities. Following that, experiment with some other techniques until they feel natural to you.

Once you begin to look, you will find synchronicities occurring all around you. As you make daily decisions, you will begin to notice that you use your intuition in ways that you never realized. Congratulate yourself. Notice how you can be in flow more often than not. This practice increases your self-awareness.

You are becoming what is known as "the intuitive person." Find joy in this sense of expanded awareness. Notice how your life can become a place of positive expectations, confidence and ease.

Intuition Can Benefit Everyone

As you have seen, intuition is accessible to everyone. Admittedly, some put it to use only negligibly, while others use it, and count on it, to live more successful and joy-filled lives. Some use it to aspire to sublime spiritual states or inspire their genius. It may appear to be bestowed on some as a gift, but it is available to all who have the desire and willingness to practice the many methods for its stimulation.

When you become fully acquainted with your own intuitive faculties and acknowledge the benefits of intuition, you can be carried far by the general processes of *asking* for what you want, *clarifying* your desires, using your *tools* to access intuition, *letting go* of the quest, having *Eureka!* moments, *acting* on your intuition and *proving* your insights. Your sincere openness to this powerful way of knowing can dramatically enhance your results.

Successfully accessing your intuition requires belief, faith, trust and a clear willingness to apply the information that you uncover intuitively. By consciously living in a way that encourages the ongoing cycles of intuition, you can attract and develop a community of friends who enjoy and acknowledge your successes. In such an atmosphere you can share your intuitions freely and enjoy applying them.

Buckminster Fuller noted that intuition is a source of truth that can be put to use to benefit everyone. Today, intuition is perhaps more important than at any time in our history. In this stage of human evolution, when technology makes every kind of information instantly available, there are not enough hours in the day for sufficient rational analysis. Decisions must be made quickly, and greater reliance must be placed on our intuitive skills. We need more innovative, and therefore more intuitive, thinkers to discover the truths and wisdom that no amount of technology can offer us. We, ourselves, need to be intuitive thinkers as we move ahead.

I am convinced that intuition is the essential ingredient in the growth of human consciousness and that all inventions and progress in every aspect of human life, from interpersonal relationships to the development of great scientific breakthroughs, are the result of intuition.
—C. Norman Shealy, M.D., Ph.D., founding president of the American Holistic Medical Association

---

In the Western world our vision of reality is changing, and this vision is transforming our civilization system-wide. More individuals are having breakthroughs and gleaning intuitive knowledge. We, as a people, are beginning to value, once again, those profound experiences that cannot be quantified, yet shape all that we hold dear in our lives. By honoring and making use of our intuition, we can see beyond the reality that we have built for ourselves and create a world filled with intuitively guided conscious choices that are of benefit to us all.

APPENDIX 1

CHAPTER REVIEW QUESTIONS

Improve your intuition by asking yourself these questions. These are also found at the end of each chapter:

CHAPTER 1 – REVIEW QUESTIONS

1. What is the one element of intuition that seems to have gained universal acceptance?

2. How is intuition immediate and direct?

3. How do you receive intuition holistically?

CHAPTER 2 – REVIEW QUESTIONS

1. What are some commonalities in thought of these writers on intuition?

2. What was the early Christian thinking about intuition?

3. What examples are there to show that intuition was not wholly embraced in these times?

CHAPTER 3 – REVIEW QUESTIONS

1. What role do Schopenhauer and Assagioli say the will has in accessing intuition?

2. According to Bergson, is it possible to use your creativity to access intuition, thereby enabling you to experience prime reality?

3. According to Jung, where does intuitive material reside?

4. What are Assagioli's thoughts on intuition?

CHAPTER 4 – REVIEW QUESTIONS

1. According to Sorokin, what are the three sources of knowledge?

2. How do reason and intuition rely upon each other?

3. According to Bahm, what should you do if you don't trust your initial intuition?

4. When have you or another experienced intuition as a warning signal?

5. What is the difference between intuition and imagination?

CHAPTER 5 – REVIEW QUESTIONS

1. In what areas does Western culture support or not support the use of intuition?

2. On what point do the mystics of both the East and West agree?

3. What is meant by Zukav's term *multisensory* human?

4. How would you describe the third eye?

CHAPTER 6 – REVIEW QUESTIONS

1. What are the five modes of reception for intuition (often called styles or levels)?

2. What is an example of each of these five modes of reception?

3. What is an example of an *exceptional* intuition?

4. What is an example of a *mediocre* intuition?

CHAPTER 7 – REVIEW QUESTIONS

1. What are several qualities of highly successful intuitive thinkers?

2. How can you develop your personal power to enhance your intuition?

3. How do traditional gender roles potentially affect intuition?

4. In what area of your life do you feel you have some expertise? How do you experience yourself as being more intuitive there?

CHAPTER 8 – REVIEW QUESTIONS

1. What is causing an increase in demand for intuition?

2. What are some key personality traits of successful intuitive business people?

3. How can management encourage intuition in the workplace?

4. What can you do to increase your intuition at work?

CHAPTER 9 – REVIEW QUESTIONS

1. How does fear keep you from accessing your intuition?

2. What other conditions potentially inhibit your intuition?

3. When has stress negatively affected your intuition?

4. How can an unrealistic self-image affect your intuition?

CHAPTER 10 – REVIEW QUESTIONS

1. What are Wallas' four stages of thought?

2. What ways could you spend time in the *incubation* stage?

3. When might an intuition appear?

4. What is the value in keeping an intuition journal?

CHAPTER 11 – REVIEW QUESTIONS

1. What are the seven steps of the *Eureka! System*?

2. What question do you have for your intuition? Use *ACT and LEAP!* to receive an answer.

3. What situation would you like solved by your intuition? Use *ACT and LEAP!* to bring you a solution.

CHAPTER 12 – REVIEW QUESTIONS

1. When have you acted on an intuition?

2. What are the three appearances of intuition?

3. What factors do you consider when evaluating another's claim to having received intuitive information?

CHAPTER 13 – REVIEW QUESTIONS

1. What desirable states of mind invite intuition?

2. What positive affirmation might be appropriate for you at this time?

3. Practice one of the breathing techniques for 3 to 5 minutes. Note how you feel before you begin and then after you finish.

4. Practice the lemon technique for yourself. Notice what you experience.

5. Practice the 10-second decisions exercises several times over the next few days. Notice what you experience.

CHAPTER 14 – REVIEW QUESTIONS

1. Why is meditation practice so foundational in intuitive work?

2. Practice the simple meditation technique a few times. What do you notice?

3. How can meditation help you break through old inhibiting beliefs?

CHAPTER 15 – REVIEW QUESTIONS

1. How does self-hypnosis differ from meditation?

2. Design a self-hypnosis session for yourself.

3. Record and then listen to the 10-Minute Self-Hypnosis Script. What was your experience?

CHAPTER 16 – REVIEW QUESTIONS

1. Practice the pre-sleep rituals, pre-sleep programming and activities upon awakening. What do you experience with this process?

2. Record a dream in your dream journal.

3. Use the Gestalt dream interpretation method to interpret your dream. What do you discover about yourself?

APPENDIX 2
RESOURCES FOR IMPROVING YOUR INTUITION

You can use the following information to support your study of intuition:

CHAPTER 13 – RESOURCES

For more examples of positive affirmations you can view the *Daily Word* published by Unity at *DailyWord.com* and *UnityOnLine.org*.

CHAPTER 14 – RESOURCES

For more information on Transcendental Meditation and to find an instructor in your area, visit *TM.org*.

For more information on the variety of meditation techniques available, you can search under meditation at the Mayo Clinic's site, *MayoClinic.com*.

CHAPTER 15 – RESOURCES

For articles on hypnosis you can visit the Mayo Clinic's site, *MayoClinic.com*.

For information on self-hypnosis, hypnosis, Transpersonal Hypnotherapy and intuition you can visit *TranspersonalInstitute.com*.

For a copy of my research study, *The Eureka Research: Experiences of Intuition in a Self-Hypnosis Experiment*, which proves that self-hypnosis can access intuition, you can visit *GoIntuition.com*.

Chapter 16 – Resources

For a comprehensive list of books on dreams and answers to common questions about dreams, you can visit the International Association for the Study of Dreams at *ASDreams.org.*

Chapter 17 – Resources

For more information on intuition and intuitive skills development, you can visit *GoIntuition.com.*

NOTES

How to Use This Book

Einstein, "Autobiographical Notes."

Part 1

Aristotle in McKeon, *Basic Works of Aristotle*, 186.

Chapter 1

Einstein, A. in "Creative Quotes and Quotations on Intuition."
  CreatingMinds.org. http://creatingminds.org/ (August 2006).
1. *Webster's Third New International Dictionary* (1976), 1187.
2. *World Book Encyclopedia, vol. 10* (1991) 355.
3. *Glossary of Epistemology/Philosophy of Science* (1993), 70.
4. *A Concise Etymological Dictionary of the English Language* (1980), 266.
5. *A Dictionary of Philosophy,* rev. 2nd ed. (1984), 177.
6. *Psychiatric Dictionary,* 6th ed. (1989), 384.
7. *Dictionary of Psychology,* 2nd rev. ed. (1985), 240.
8. *The Penguin Dictionary of Psychology* (1985), 373.
9. Goldberg, *The Intuitive Edge.*
10. *Webster's Third New International Dictionary* (1976), s.v. "truth."
11. *Merriam-Webster Dictionary* (1994), s.v. "knowledge," "wisdom,"
  "understanding," "[to] understand."
12. *One psychiatrist.... Another psychiatrist.... One educational researcher...*
  namely Jung... Berne... Wild... Bastick—Hall and Nordby, *A Primer of
  Jungian Psychology*; Berne, "The Nature of Intuition;" Wild, *Intuition*;
  Bastick, *Intuition.*
13. *A psychiatrist...* namely Assagioli—Assagioli, *The Act of Will.*
14. *And a mystic...* namely Sri Aurobindo—Satprem, *Sri Aurobindo.*
15. *Psychiatric Dictionary,* s.v. "unconscious."
16. Ibid.
17. Ibid., s.v. "preconscious."
18. *referring to intuition as a preconscious process...* is Bastick—
  Bastick, *Intuition.*
19. *The superconscious...* according to Assagioli—Assagioli, *The Act of Will.*
20. *or superconscient...* according to Sri Aurobindo—Satprem, *Sri Aurobindo.*
21. *One thinker...* namely Assagioli—Assagioli, *The Act of Will.*
22. *It also flows through intuitive channels...* according to Zukav—Zukav,
  Seat of the Soul, 77-90.
23. Rama, Ballentine, and Ajaya, *Yoga and Psychotherapy.*
24. Gerber, *Vibrational Medicine.*
25. *The Holy Bible,* Mathew 6:22.
26. Yogananda, *Autobiography of a Yogi,* 179-180.
27. *One, for example.... Others...* namely Assagioli, Rama, Ballentine, and
  Ajaya—Assagioli, *Psychosynthesis*; Rama, Ballentine, and Ajaya, *Yoga
  and Psychotherapy.*

Chapter 2

Socrates in Plato, "Apology" (sct. 21).
1. Noddings and Shore, *Awakening the Inner Eye*, 6.
2. Plato, *Plato in Twelve Volumes*.
3. Aristotle, in McKeon, *The Basic Works of Aristotle*, 186.
4. Archimedes, in Bartlett, *Familiar Quotations*, 83.
5. Plutarch, *Plutarch's Complete Works*, 490.
6. May, *The Courage to Create*, 112.
7. Plotinus, "Enneads III," 397.
8. Randall, *The Career of Philosophy*.
9. Leff, *Medieval Thought*.
10. Noddings and Shore, *Awakening the Inner Eye*.
11. Williams, *Saint Bernard of Clairvaux*.
12. *New Catholic Encyclopedia*, vol. 5.; Copleston, *History of Philosophy*, vol. 3; Noddings and Shore, *Awakening the Inner Eye*.
13. Leff, *Medieval Thought*.
14. Ockham, in "Sentences" in Copleston, *History of Philosophy* 3:62.
15. Ockham, in "Quodlibeta" in Copleston, *History of Philosophy* 3:64.
16. Sorokin, *The Crisis of Our Age*.
17. Achterberg, *Imagery in Healing*.
18. Noddings and Shore, *Awakening the Inner Eye*.
19. McCann, *Nostradamus*.
20. Descartes, *The Philosophical Works* 1:7, 33–34.
21. Descartes, in "Oeuvres de Descartes" 5:136 in Randall, *The Career of Philosophy*, 388.
22. Spinoza, *The Collected Works*, 41.
23. Ibid., 490.
24. Noddings and Shore, *Awakening the Inner Eye*.
25. *World Book Encyclopedia*, 1991, s.v. "Age of Rationalism," "Romanticism," "Jean-Jacques Rousseau."
26. Rousseau, *Emile*.
27. Kant, *Critique of Pure Reason* (Smith, trans.), 93.
28. Kant, *Critique of Pure Reason* (Smith, trans.).

Chapter 3

Assagioli, *Psychosynthesis*, 221.
1. Fox, *Schopenhauer*.
2. Ibid., 88, 186.
3. James, *The Varieties of Religious Experience*, 300.
4. Rothberg, "Theories of Inquiry."
5. Bergson, *Creative Evolution*.
6. Ibid., 292.
7. Westcott, *Toward a Contemporary Psychology of Intuition*.
8. Croce, *Benedetto Croce's Poetry and Literature*.
9. Ibid.
10. Piccoli, *Benedetto Croce: An Introduction*, 114.

11. Westcott, *Toward a Contemporary Psychology of Intuition*.
12. Ibid., 16.
13. Harman and Rheingold, *Higher Creativity*.
14. Jung, *Psychological Types*.
15. Jung, *Psychology and Religion*, 41.
16. Hall and Nordby, *A Primer of Jungian Psychology*.
17. Jung, *Psychological Types*.
18. Ibid.
19. Westcott, *Toward a Contemporary Psychology of Intuition*, 34–35.
20. Wild, *Intuition*; Westcott, *Toward a Contemporary Psychology of Intuition*.
21. *Encyclopedia of Psychology*.
22. Hall and Nordby, *A Primer of Jungian Psychology*.
23. Harman and Rheingold, *Higher Creativity*.
24. Assagioli, *The Act of Will*.
25. Assagioli, *Psychosynthesis*.
26. Ibid., 217.
27. Assagioli, *The Act of Will*.
28. Assagioli, *Psychosynthesis*, 217.
29. Assagioli, *The Act of Will*.
30. Ibid., 195–196.
31. Berne, "The Nature of Intuition," 205.
32. Das and Gorman, *How Can I Help?*, 94.
33. Einstein, "Autobiographical Notes."
34. Fuller, *Intuition*, 58.
35. Ibid.

CHAPTER 4

Mitchell, E. in "Top 10 Quotations about Intuition."
    TopTen.org. http://topten.org/ (August 2006).
1. Parikh, Neubauer and Lank, *Intuition*, 38.
2. Wild, *Intuition*, 224.
3. Ibid., 226.
4. Winkler, *Man: The Bridge Between Two Worlds*, 218.
5. Sorokin, *The Crisis of Our Age*, 105.
6. Westcott, *Toward a Contemporary Psychology of Intuition*, 19.
7. Ibid., 17.
8. Ibid.
9. Ibid.
10. Bahm, *Types of Intuition*, 1.
11. Westcott, *Toward a Contemporary Psychology of Intuition*, 19.
12. Bahm, *Types of Intuition*, 16, 44.
13. Ibid., 7.
14. Bowers, "Intuition and Discovery."
15. *Encyclopedia of Psychology*.
16. Bruner, *The Process of Education* (1961), 13; Westcott, *Toward a Contemporary Psychology of Intuition*, 39.
17. Westcott, *Toward a Contemporary Psychology of Intuition*, 41.

18. Bruner, *The Process of Education* (1960); Westcott, *Toward a Contemporary Psychology of Intuition.*
19. Bastick, *Intuition*, 25.
20. Ibid., 298.
21. Ibid.
22. Ibid.
23. *Webster's Third New International Dictionary* (1976), s.v. "creative."
24. Sorokin, *The Crisis of Our Age.*
25. Wonder and Blake, "Creativity East and West," 183–184.
26. Noddings and Shore, *Awakening the Inner Eye*, 57.
27. Ibid., 60.
28. Murray, *Artwork of the Mind*, 2.
29. Ibid.
30. Bastick, *Intuition*, 25.
31. *Webster's Third New International Dictionary* (1976), s.v. "insight."
32. de Becker, *The Gift of Fear*, 91.
33. Vaughan, *Awakening Intuition*, 185.
34. Koestler, *The Act of Creation*, 208.
35. Harman and Rheingold, *Higher Creativity.*
36. Rowan, *The Intuitive Manager.*
37. Agor, "How Intuition Can Be Used."
38. Cappon, "The Anatomy of Intuition."

CHAPTER 5

Lao-Tsu in "Intuition Quotes and Quotations." NonStopEnglish.com. http://nonstopenglish.com/ (August 2006).
1. Wonder and Blake, "Creativity East and West."
2. Vaughan, *Awakening Intuition*, 49–50.
3. Ibid.
4. Ibid.
5. Ibid., 199, 191.
6. Satprem, *Sri Aurobindo*, 206.
7. Ibid., 217.
8. Ibid.
9. Ibid., 218.
10. Ibid., 220.
11. Yogananda, *Autobiography of a Yogi*, 177, 178.
12. Das and Gorman, *How Can I Help?*, 109.
13. Ibid., 111.
14. Rama, Ballentine, and Ajaya, *Yoga and Psychotherapy.*
15. Ibid., 265.
16. Ibid.
17. Myss, *Anatomy of the Spirit*; Zukav, *The Seat of the Soul.*
18. Zukav, 88.
19. Ibid., 80.
20. Association for Research and Enlightenment, *Intuition, Visions, and Dreams*, 1.
21. Rama, Ballentine, and Ajaya, *Yoga and Psychotherapy*, 269.

22. Gerber, Vibrational Medicine, 128.
23. Ibid., 374.
24. Rama, Ballentine, and Ajaya, *Yoga and Psychotherapy.*
25. Murray, *A History of Western Psychology.*
26. Association for Research and Enlightenment, *Meditation,* 2.
27. Schwarz, *Human Energy Systems;* Schwarz, *Voluntary Controls.*
28. Myss and Shealy, *Science of Medical Intuition,* 18.
29. Rockenstein, "Intuitive Processes," 78.
30. Vogel, "Scientists Probe Feelings."

PART 2

Salk, J. in *The Speaker's Electronic Reference Collection.* A Apex Software, 1994.

CHAPTER 6

Ray, "Sharing the Wisdom," 295.
1. Rosanoff, *Intuition Workout.*
2. Agor, *The Logic of Intuitive Decision Making.*
3. Vaughan, *Awakening Intuition,* 67.
4. Ibid.
5. Emery, *Intuition Workbook.*
6. Goldberg, *The Intuitive Edge,* 77.
7. Goldberg, *The Intuitive Edge.*
8. Strunz, "Preconscious Mental Activity;" Weisberg, *Creativity.*
9. Krippner and Dillard, *Dreamworking.*
10. Ibid., 81–82.
11. Keats, *Letter to John Taylor,* 135.

CHAPTER 7

Carrell, A. in *Poor Man's College Quotations Collection*, ed. Sidney Madwed. A Apex Software, 1994.
1. Bushe and Gibbs, "Predicting Organization Development Consulting Competence."
2. Goldberg, *The Intuitive Edge.*
3. Bruner, *The Process of Education* (1960).
4. Hanson, in Goldberg, *The Intuitive Edge,* 104.
5. Cappon, "The Anatomy of Intuition;" Jung, *Psychological Types.*
6. Cappon, "The Anatomy of Intuition."
7. Westcott, *Toward a Contemporary Psychology of Intuition,* 101.
8. Ibid.
9. Goldberg, *The Intuitive Edge.*
10. Boden, *Creative Mind.*
11. Schermerhorn, *Management for Productivity.*
12. Kant, *Critique of Pure Reason* (Muller, trans.), from prefatory note.
13. Sullivan, "Portrait of a Prophet," 81.
14. Ibid.
15. Myss, *Anatomy of the Spirit, 186.*

16. Myss, *Anatomy of the Spirit;* Vaughan, *Awakening Intuition.*
17. Goldberg, *The Intuitive Edge;* Harman and Rheingold, *Higher Creativity;* Achterberg, *Imagery in Healing.*
18. Myss, *Anatomy of the Spirit,* 38, 52.
19. Goldberg, *The Intuitive Edge.*
20. Fisher, *Intuition.*
21. Vaughan, *Awakening Intuition.*
22. Welles, "A Qualitative Study of Intuitive Processes."
23. Miller, *The Creative Edge.*
24. Dial, "Creativity 101."
25. Miller, *The Creative Edge.*
26. *Webster's Third New International Dictionary* (1976), s.v. "creativity."
27. Richards, Kinney, Benet, and Merzel, "Assessing Everyday Creativity."
28. Csikszentmihalyi, *The Evolving Self,* 175.
29. Richards et al., "Assessing Everyday Creativity;" Goleman, "A New Index."
30. Goleman, "A New Index."
31. Goldberg, *The Intuitive Edge,* 104.
32. Benderly, "Everyday Intuition."
33. Agor, *Intuitive Management* and *The Logic of Intuitive Decision Making.*

CHAPTER 8

Kerkorian, K. in "Business Quotes." Woopidoo.com.
   http://woopidoo.com/ (August 2006).
Iacocca, L. in "Top 10 Quotations about Intuition." TopTen.org.
   http://topten.org/ (August 2006).
Winfrey, O. in *The Ultimate Success Quotations Library,* 1997.
Hilton, C. in "Top 10 Quotations about Intuition." TopTen.org.
   http://topten.org/ (August 2006).
Peters and Waterman, *In Search of Excellence,* 63.
1. Peters, in *Fast Company* (March 2001), in Wanless, *Intuition at Work,* 23.
2. *Adam Smith's Moneyworld,* 21.
3. Rosanoff, "Making the Workplace Safe for Intuition," 217.
4. Ray, "Sharing the Wisdom," 292.
5. Ibid.
6. Agor, *Intuitive Management* and *The Logic of Intuitive Decision Making.*
7. Parikh, Neubauer and Lank, *Intuition.*
8. Rowan, *The Intuitive Manager,* 61, 146.
9. Harper, "Intuition: What Separates Executives from Managers," 31, 5.
10. Miller, *The Creative Edge.*
11. Goldberg, *The Intuitive Edge;* Krishnamurti, *Think on These Things;* Vaughan, *Awakening Intuition;* Zukav, *Seat of the Soul.*
12. Raudsepp, "Can You Trust Your Hunches?"
13. Agor, *Intuitive Management;* Agor, *The Logic of Intuitive Decision Making;* Vaughan, *Awakening Intuition;* Goldberg, *The Intuitive Edge.*
14. Miller, *The Creative Edge;* Koestler, *The Act of Creation;* Fisher, *Intuition;* Rowan, *The Intuitive Manager;* Harman and Rheingold, *Higher Creativity.*
15. Miller, *The Creative Edge;* Goldberg, *The Intuitive Edge;* Fisher, *Intuition.*

16. Ray, "Sharing the Wisdom," 295.
17. Tecker, Eide and Frankel in Salisbury, "Sharpening Your Sixth Sense," 40.
18. Ray, "Sharing the Wisdom," 295.
19. *Harvard Business Review* (Jan.-Feb. 1994).
20. Mintzberg, *Managers Not MBAs*, 10.
21. Salisbury, "Sharpening Your Sixth Sense," 40.

CHAPTER 9

Nehru, J. in "The Ultimate Success Quotations Library."
   Cybernation.com. http://cybernation.org/, (1997).
1. Kautz, in Sullivan, "Portrait of a Prophet."
2. Zukav, *Seat of the Soul.*
3. Goldberg, *The Intuitive Edge.*
4. Rosanoff, *Intuition Workout.*
5. Agor, *Intuitive Management;* Vaughan, *Awakening Intuition.*
6. Emery, *Intuition Workbook.*
7. Ibid.; Goldberg, *The Intuitive Edge*; Markley, "Using Depth Intuition;"
   Miller, *The Creative Edge;* Parikh, Neubauer, and Lank, *Intuition;*
   Raudsepp, "Can You Trust Your Hunches?;" Rowan, *The Intuitive
   Manager.*
8. Goldberg, *The Intuitive Edge*; Miller, *The Creative Edge;* Rowan,
   The Intuitive Manager.
9. Rockenstein, "Intuitive Processes," 79.
10. Haddock, "10 Keys to Greater Creativity;" Miller, *The Creative Edge.*
11. Goldberg, *The Intuitive Edge.*
12. Fisher, *Intuition;* Miller, *The Creative Edge.*
13. Goldberg, *The Intuitive Edge.*
14. Wonder and Blake, "Creativity East and West."
15. Assagioli, *Psychosynthesis,* 217.
16. Rowan, *The Intuitive Manager.*
17. Krishnamurti, *Think on These Things,* 77.
18. Goldberg, *The Intuitive Edge;* Agor, *The Logic of Intuitive Decision
   Making.*
19. de Becker, *The Gift of Fear.*
20. Goldberg, *The Intuitive Edge;* Miller, *The Creative Edge.*
21. Haddock, "10 Keys to Greater Creativity."
22. Miller, *The Creative Edge;* Vaughan, *Awakening Intuition.*
23. Emery, *Intuition Workbook.*
24. Vaughan, *Awakening Intuition.*
25. Haddock, "10 Keys to Greater Creativity."
26. Vaughan, *Awakening Intuition.*
27. Association for Research and Enlightenment, *Intuition, Visions, and Dreams.*
28. Agor, *Intuitive Management* and *The Logic of Intuitive Decision Making;*
   Miller, *The Creative Edge;* Rowan, *The Intuitive Manager.*
29. Goleman, "A New Index."
30. Yogananda, *Autobiography of a Yogi.*
31. Rowan, *The Intuitive Manager.*

32. Schwab, "No Static in Your Attic," 256.
33. Vaughan, *Awakening Intuition.*
34. Miller, *The Creative Edge.*
35. Goldberg, *The Intuitive Edge.*
36. Miller, *The Creative Edge.*
37. Rowan, *The Intuitive Manager.*
38. Agor, *Intuitive Management.*
39. Rowan, *The Intuitive Manager.*
40. Agor, *The Logic of Intuitive Decision Making;* Vaughan, *Awakening Intuition.*
41. Emery, *Intuition Workbook.*
42. Haddock, "10 Keys to Greater Creativity;" May, *The Courage to Create.*
43. Rowan, *The Intuitive Manager.*
44. Das and Gorman, *How Can I Help?;* Krishnamurti, *Think on These Things;* Miller, *The Creative Edge;* Raudsepp, "Can You Trust Your Hunches?"
45. A. Campbell, "Brief Case."
46. Rowan, *The Intuitive Manager.*
47. Shealy, August 1998 interview with the author.

CHAPTER 10

Bergman, I. in *The Speaker's Electronic Reference Collection,* AApex Software, 1994.
1. Wallas, *The Art of Thought;* Dial, "Creativity 101;" Harman and Rheingold, *Higher Creativity;* Markley, "Using Depth Intuition;" Murphy, *Human Potentialities*; Rockenstein, "Intuitive Processes."
2. Wallas, *The Art of Thought.*
3. Ibid., 11.
4. Wallas, *The Art of Thought.*
5. Fisher, *Intuition.*
6. Goldberg, *The Intuitive Edge;* Wallas, *The Art of Thought.*
7. Goldberg, *The Intuitive Edge,* 163.
8. Fisher, *Intuition;* Vaughan, *Awakening Intuition;* Koestler, *The Act of Creation.*
9. Koestler, *The Act of Creation;* Fisher, *Intuition;* Goldberg, *The Intuitive Edge;* Harman and Rheingold, *Higher Creativity;* Miller, *The Creative Edge;* Rowan, *The Intuitive Manager;* Vaughan, *Awakening Intuition.*
10. Wallas, *The Art of Thought.*
11. Goldberg, *The Intuitive Edge.*
12. Vaughan, *Awakening Intuition;* Goldberg, *The Intuitive Edge;* Myss, *Anatomy of the Spirit;* Harman and Rheingold, *Higher Creativity;* Achterberg, *Imagery in Healing.*
13. Fisher, *Intuition.*
14. Dean and Mihalsky, *Executive ESP.*
15. James, *The Varieties of Religious Experience,* 101–102.
16. Goldberg, *The Intuitive Edge.*
17. Vaughan, *Awakening Intuition;* Fisher, *Intuition;* Myss, *Anatomy of the Spirit.*
18. Ampère, in Koestler, *The Act of Creation,* 117.
19. Goldberg, *The Intuitive Edge,* 202.
20. Bastick, *Intuition.*

21. Rosanoff, "Making the Workplace Safe for Intuition," 222.
22. Goldberg, *The Intuitive Edge;* Fisher, *Intuition.*
23. Vaughan, *Awakening Intuition.*
24. Fisher, *Intuition;* Vaughan, *Awakening Intuition.*
25. Murphy, *Human Potentialities,* 130–131.
26. Harman and Rheingold, *Higher Creativity,* xxii.
27. Harman and Rheingold, *Higher Creativity.*
28. Ibid., 24, 25.
29. Harman and Rheingold, *Higher Creativity.*

PART 3
Mishlove, "What is Intuition?" 14.

CHAPTER 11
Assagioli, *The Act of Will,* 196.

CHAPTER 12
Chopra, D. *The Seven Spiritual Laws of Success,* 89.
1. Assagioli, *The Act of Will;* Assagioli, *Psychosynthesis.*
2. Bach, in Harman and Rheingold, *Higher Creativity,* 33; Sorokin, *The Crisis of Our Age,* 110.
3. Mozart, in Goldberg, *The Intuitive Edge,* 68, 70.
4. Goldberg, *The Intuitive Edge,* 71.

PART 4
Bell, A. G. in "Top 10 Quotations about Intuition." TopTen.org. http://topten.org/ (August 2006).

CHAPTER 13
Salk, J., in "The Ultimate Success Quotations Library." Cybernation.com. http://cybernation.org/, (1997).
1. Yogananda, *Autobiography of a Yogi.*
2. Vaughan, *Awakening Intuition,* 13.
3. Goldberg, *The Intuitive Edge,* 186, 188.
4. Cayce, in Association for Research and Enlightenment, *Meditation,* 3.
5. Harman and Rheingold, *Higher Creativity;* Jacobson, *Progressive Relaxation; Encyclopedia of Psychology* 1:129, 1:242, 3:220, 3:286.
6. *Encyclopedia of Psychology* 3:286.
7. Harman and Rheingold, *Higher Creativity.*
8. Achterberg, *Imagery in Healing.*
9. Benson and Klipper, *The Relaxation Response; Encyclopedia of Psychology* 3:220, 3: 286; Harman and Rheingold, *Higher Creativity.*
10. Goldberg, *The Intuitive Edge.*
11. Trivieri, Jr. and American Holistic Medical Association, *Guide to Holistic Health,* 129.

12. Maltz, *Psycho-Cybernetics.*
13. Rico, *Writing the Natural Way,* 35, 36.
14. Goldberg, *The Intuitive Edge.*
15. Fisher, *Intuition.*

CHAPTER 14

Yogananda, *The Law of Success,* 24.
Bloomfield, Cain and Jaffe, *TM: Discovering Inner Energy,* 10.
Tweed and Prothero, *Asian Religions in America,* 241.
1. Goldberg, *The Intuitive Edge;* Vaughan, *Awakening Intuition;* Fisher, *Intuition;*
   Emery, *Intuition Workbook;* Agor, *Intuitive Management.*
2. Vaughan, *Awakening Intuition,* 11.
3. Tweed and Prothero, *Asian Religions in America.*
4. Keats, *Letter to John Taylor,* 289.
5. Carlyle, "Characteristics," 297.

CHAPTER 15

Salk, J., in *Isaac Asimov's Book of Science and Nature Quotations,* ed.
   Jason Shulman & Isaac Asimov, 1988.
Cheek, *Hypnosis,* 59.
Mayo Clinic, "Hypnosis," (April 2007).
1. Salisbury, *Determining Possible Incidents of Intuition.*
2. Johnson, "Self-Hypnosis: Behavioral and Phenomenological."
3. Fromm, Brown, Hurt, Oberlander, Boxer, and Pfeifer. "The Phenomena and
   Characteristics of Self-Hypnosis."
4. *Federal Dictionary of Occupational Titles,* "Hypnotherapist 079.157.010."
5. Sue and Sue, *Understanding Abnormal Behavior.*
6. Waldholz, "Altered States – Hypnosis Goes Mainstream."
7. Spiegel, in Waldholz.
8. Salisbury, *Transpersonal Hypnotherapy Institute Catalog;* Hasegawa and
   Salisbury, *Transpersonal Hypnotherapy Workbook.*
9. Wallas, *The Art of Thought.*
10. Tellegen and Atkinson, "Openness to Absorbing and Self-Altering Experiences."
11. Edmonston, "Anesis."
12. Kirsch, Lynn, and Rhue, "Introduction to Clinical Hypnosis."
13. Wallas, *The Art of Thought.*
14. Fisher, *Intuition,* 121.
15. Agor, *Intuitive Management.*
16. Vaughan, *Awakening Intuition.*
17. Salisbury, *Transpersonal Hypnotherapy Institute Catalog;* Hasegawa and
    Salisbury, *Transpersonal Hypnotherapy Workbook.*

CHAPTER 16

Descartes, in Krippner and Dillard, *Dreamworking,* 73.
1. Krippner and Dillard, *Dreamworking,* 120.
2. LaBerge and Rheingold, *Exploring the World of Lucid Dreaming.*
3. Krippner and Dillard, *Dreamworking;* Vaughan, *Awakening Intuition.*
4. Vaughan, *Awakening Intuition.*
5. Jung, *Man and His Symbols,* 53.
6. Goldberg, *The Intuitive Edge;* Vaughan, *Awakening Intuition;* Fisher, *Intuition.*
7. Perls, *The Gestalt Approach.*
8. Vaughan *Awakening Intuition, 121.*

CHAPTER 17

Lao-Tsu in Mitchell, *Tao Te Ching*, 33.
Bergson, "Introduction to Metaphysics."
Shealy and Myss, *The Creation of Health*, xxii.
1. Haddock, "10 Keys to Greater Creativity."
2. Britton, "You Are Creative."

BIBLIOGRAPHY

A Concise Etymological Dictionary of the English Language. New York: G. P. Putnam's Sons, 1980.

A Dictionary of Philosophy. 2nd ed. rev. New York: St. Martin's Press, 1984.

Achterberg, J. *Imagery in Healing: Shamanism and Modern Medicine.* Boston: Shambala, 1985.

Adam Smith's Moneyworld, 21 November 1987.

Agor, W. *Intuitive Management: Integrating Left and Right Brain Management Skills.* Englewood Cliffs, NJ: Prentice-Hall, 1984.

———. *The Logic of Intuitive Decision Making.* New York: Quorum Books, 1986.

———. "How Intuition Can Be Used to Enhance Creativity in Organizations." *Journal of Creative Behavior* 25, no. 1 (1991): 11-20.

Assagioli, R. *Psychosynthesis: A Manual of Principles and Techniques.* New York: Hobbs, Dorman & Company, 1965.

———. *The Act of Will.* New York: Penguin Group, 1974.

Association for Research and Enlightenment. *Commentary: A New Look at the Edgar Cayce Readings on Intuition, Visions, and Dreams.* Virginia Beach, VA, December 1987.

———. *Commentary: A New Look at the Edgar Cayce Readings on Meditation.* Virginia Beach, VA, October 1987.

———. *Intuition, Visions, and Dreams.* Virginia Beach, VA, 1976.

Bahm, A. J. *Types of Intuition.* Albuquerque: University of New Mexico Press, 1960.

Bartlett, J. *Familiar Quotations,* 16th ed. Boston: Little Brown and Co., 1992.

Bastick, T. *Intuition: How We Think and Act.* New York: John Wiley & Sons, 1982.

Benderly, B. L. "Everyday Intuition." *Psychology Today,* September 1989, 35-40.

Benson, H., and M. Klipper. *The Relaxation Response.* New York: Avon, 1975.

Bergson, H. *Creative Evolution.* Translated by A. Mitchell. New York: Random House, 1944.

Bergson, H. "Introduction to Metaphysics." 1903 repr. in *The Creative Mind,* 1946.

Berne, E. "The Nature of Intuition." *Psychiatric Quarterly* 23 (1949): 203-226.

Bloomfield, H. H., M. P. Cain and D. T. Jaffe. *TM: Discovering Inner Energy and Overcoming Stress,* New York: Delacorte Press, 1975.

Boden, M. A. *Creative Mind: Myths and Mechanisms.* New York: Basic Books, 1991.

Bowers, K. S. "Intuition and Discovery." in *Theories of the Unconscious and Theories of the Self,* edited by R. Stern, 71-90. Hillsdale, NJ: Analytic Press, 1987.

Britton, M. "You Are Creative." *Science of Mind* 67, no. 5 (1994): 20-23.

Bruner, J. S. *The Process of Education.* Cambridge, MA: Harvard University Press, 1960.

———. *The Process of Education.* New York: Vintage Books, 1961.

Bushe, G. R., and B. W. Gibbs. "Predicting Organization Development Consulting Competence from the Myers-Briggs Type Indicator and Stage of Ego Development." *Journal of Applied Behavioral Science* 26, no. 3 (1990): 337-367.

Buzan, T. *Using Both Sides of Your Brain*. New York: NAL/Dutton, 1983.

Campbell, A. "Brief Case: Strategy and Intuition—A Conversation with Henry Mintzberg." *Long Range Planning* 24, no. 2 (1991): 108-110.

Campbell, J. *The Hero with a Thousand Faces*. Princeton, NJ: Princeton University Press, 1973.

Cappon, D. "The Anatomy of Intuition." *Psychology Today*, May/June 1993, 41-45, 86, 90, 94.

Carlyle, T. "Characteristics." In *Critical and Miscellaneous Essays*. New York: D. Appleton & Co., 1870.

Cheek, D. *Hypnosis: The Application of Ideomotor Techniques*, Boston: Allyn and Bacon, 1994, 59.

Chopra, D. *The Seven Spiritual Laws of Success*. Novato, CA: New World Library, 1994.

Copleston, F. *History of Philosophy*. Vol. 3. Westminster, MD: Newman Press, 1959.

Croce, B. *Benedetto Croce's Poetry and Literature: An Introduction to Its Criticism and History*. Translated by G. Gullace. Carbondale, IL: Southern Illinois University Press, 1981.

Csikszentmihalyi, M. *The Evolving Self: A Psychology for the Third Millennium*. New York: Harper Perennial, 1994.

Das, R., and P. Gorman. *How Can I Help? Stories and Reflections on Service*. New York: Alfred A Knopf, 1995.

Dean, D. and J. Mihalsky. *Executive ESP*. Englewood Cliffs, NJ: Prentice Hall, 1974.

de Becker, G. *The Gift of Fear*. Boston: Little Brown, 1997.

Descartes, R. *The Philosophical Works of Decartes, in Two Volumes*. Vol. 1. Translated by E. S. Haldane and G. R. Ross. Cambridge: Cambridge University Press, 1968.

Dial, J. "Creativity 101: Let's Legislate It." *Journal of Creative Behavior* 25, no. 3 (1991): 241-243.

Dictionary of Psychology. 2nd rev. ed. New York: Bantam Doubleday Dell Publishing Group, 1985.

Edmonston, W. "Anesis." In *Theories of Hypnosis: Current Models and Perspectives*, edited by S. J. Lynn and J. W. Rhue, 197-237. New York: Guilford Press, 1991.

Einstein, A. "Autobiographical Notes." *Albert Einstein: Philosopher-Scientist*, edited by P. A. Schlipp, 2-94. Evanston, IL: Library of Living, 1946.

Emery, M. *Intuition Workbook: An Expert's Guide to Unlocking the Wisdom of Your Unconscious Mind*. Englewood Cliffs, NJ: Prentice Hall, 1994.

Encyclopedia of Psychology. 3 vols. New York: John Wiley & Sons, 1984.

Federal Dictionary of Occupational Titles, "Hypnotherapist 079.157.010." Washington, DC: United States Department of Labor.

Fisher, M. *Intuition: How to Use It in Your Life*. Green Farms, CT: Wildcat Publishing, 1995.

Fox, M., ed. *Schopenhauer: His Philosophical Achievement*. Sussex: Harvester Press, 1980.

Fromm, E., D. P. Brown, S. W. Hurt, J. Z. Oberlander, A. M. Boxer, and G. Pfeifer. "The Phenomena and Characteristics of Self-Hypnosis." *International Journal of Clinical and Experimental Hypnosis* 29 (1981): 189-246.

Fuller, R. B. *Intuition*. Garden City, NY: Doubleday, 1972.

Gendlin, E. T. *Focusing*. New York: Bantam Books, 1981.

Gerber, R. *Vibrational Medicine: The #1 Handbook of Subtle-Energy Therapies*. 3rd ed. Rochester, VT: Bear and Company, 2001.

Glossary of Epistemology/Philosophy of Science. New York: Paragon House, 1993.

Goldberg, P. *The Intuitive Edge*. New York: G. P. Putnam's Sons, 1983.

Goleman, D. "A New Index Illuminates the Creative Life." *New York Times*, September 13, 1988, sec. C.

Haddock, P. "10 Keys to Greater Creativity." *Science of Mind* 67, no. 5 (1994): 12-19.

Hall, C. S., and V. J. Nordby. *A Primer of Jungian Psychology*. New York: Mentor, 1973.

Harman, W., and H Rheingold. *Higher Creativity: Liberating the Unconscious for Breakthrough Insights*. Los Angeles: Jeremy P. Tarcher, 1984.

Harper, S. C. "Intuition: What Separates Executives from Managers." *Business Horizons*, Sept.-Oct. 1988, 31, 5.

Harvard Business Review. "The Rise and Fall of Strategic Planning." Jan.-Feb. 1994.

Hasegawa, Y., and A. F. Salisbury. *The Transpersonal Hypnotherapy Workbook*. Golden, CO: Transpersonal Hypnotherapy Institute, 1995.

Jacobson, E. *Progressive Relaxation*. Chicago: University of Chicago Press, 1929.

James, W. *The Varieties of Religious Experience: A Study in Human Nature*. New York: Macmillan, 1961.

Johnson, L. S. "Self-Hypnosis: Behavioral and Phenomenological Comparisons with Heterohypnosis." *International Journal of Clinical and Experimental Hypnosis* 27, no. 3 (1979): 240-264.

Jung, C. G. *Man and His Symbols*. Garden City, NY: Doubleday, 1964.

———. *Psychological Types or the Psychology of Individuation*. New York: Harcourt, Brace, 1938.

———. *Psychology and Religion: West and East*. In *Collected Works II*. New York: Princeton University Press, 1958.

Kant, I. *Immanuel Kant's Critique of Pure Reason*. Translated by N. Kemp Smith. New York: St Martin's Press, 1965.

Keats, J. "Letter to John Taylor, Hampstead, February 27, 1818." *The Complete Poetical Works and Letters of John Keats*. Boston: Houghton Mifflin Company, 1899.

Kirsch, I., S. J. Lynn, and J. W. Rhue. "Introduction to Clinical Hypnosis." *Handbook of Clinical Hypnosis*, edited by J. W. Rhue, S. J. Lynn, and I. Kirsch, 3-22. Washington, DC: American Psychological Association, 1993.

Koestler, A. *The Act of Creation*. New York: Penguin Books, 1964.

Krippner, S., and J. Dillard. *Dreamworking: How to Use Your Dreams for Creative Problem-Solving.* Buffalo, NY: Bearly Limited, 1988.

Krishnamurti, J. *Think on These Things.* New York: Harper Perennial, 1989.

LaBerge, S., and H. Rheingold. *Exploring the World of Lucid Dreaming.* New York: Ballantine Books, 1990.

Leadbeater, C. W. *The Chakras.* Wheaton, IL: Theosophical Publishing House, 1977.

Leff, G. *Medieval Thought: St. Augustine to Ockham.* Baltimore: Penguin Books, 1970.

Maltz, M. *Psycho-Cybernetics.* New York: Pocket Books, 1969.

Markley, O. W. "Using Depth Intuition in Creative Problem Solving." *Journal of Creative Behavior* 22, no. 2 (1988): 85-100.

May, R. *The Courage to Create.* New York: Bantam Books, 1978.

Mayo Clinic, "Hypnosis: An Altered State of Consciousness." MayoClinic.com/health/hypnosis/SA00084 (April 2007).

McCann, L. *Nostradamus: The Man Who Saw through Time.* New York: Creative Age Press, 1941.

McKeon, R., ed. *The Basic Works of Aristotle.* New York: Random House, 1941.

McKim, R. H. "Relaxed Attention." *Journal of Creative Behavior* 8, no.1 (1974): 265-275.

Miller, W. *The Creative Edge: Fostering Innovation Where You Work.* Reading, MA: Addison-Wesley Publishing, 1987.

Mintzberg, H. *Managers Not MBAs: A Hard Look at the Soft Practice of Managing and Management Development.* San Francisco: Berrett-Koehler Publishers, Inc., 2004.

Mishlove, J. "What is Intuition?" *Intuition at Work: Pathways to Unlimited Possibilities.* San Francisco: New Leaders Press/Sterling & Stone Ltd., 1996, 14.

Mitchell, S., *Tao Te Ching: A New English Version.* New York: Harper & Row, 1988.

Murphy, G. *Human Potentialities.* New York: Basic Books, 1958.

Murray, D. J., *A History of Western Psychology.* Englewood Cliffs, NJ: Prentice Hall, 1988.

Murray, M., *Artwork of the Mind: An Interdisciplinary Description of Insight and the Search for It in Student Writing.* Cresskill, NJ: Hampton Press, 1995.

Myss, C. *Anatomy of the Spirit.* New York: Harmony Books, 1996.

Myss, C. and N. Shealy. *The Science of Medical Intuition: Self-Diagnosis and Healing with Your Body's Energy Systems.* Boulder, CO: Sounds True, 2002.

New Catholic Encyclopedia. Vol. 5. New York: McGraw-Hill Book Co., 1967.

Noddings, N., and P. J. Shore. *Awakening the Inner Eye: Intuition in Education.* New York: Teachers College, Columbia University, 1984.

Osborn, A. *Applied Imagination.* New York: Scribner's, 1953.

Palmer, H., ed. *Inner Knowing.* New York: Jeremy P. Tarcher/Putnam, 1998.

Parikh, J., F. Neubauer, and A. Lank. *Intuition: The New Frontier of Management.* Cambridge, MA: Blackwell Business, 1994.

Perls, F. *The Gestalt Approach and Eye Witness to Therapy.* US: Science and Behavior Books, Inc., 1973.

Peters, T. J., and R. H. Waterman Jr. *In Search of Excellence: Lessons from America's Best-Run Companies.* New York: Harper & Row, 1982.

Piccoli, R. *Benedetto Croce: An Introduction to His Philosophy.* New York: Harcourt, Brace & Co., 1922.

Plato. "Euthyphro;" "Apology;" "Crito;" 'Phaedo;" "Phaedrus." *Plato in Twelve Volumes.* Vol. 1. Translated by H. N. Fowler. Cambridge, MA: Harvard University Press, 1977.

Plotinus. "Enneads III." *Plotinus in Six Volumes.* Vol. 3:1-9. Cambridge, MA: Harvard University Press, 1967.

Plutarch. *Essays and Miscellanies.* Vol. 3, *Plutarch's Complete Works.* New York: Wheeler Publishing Co., 1909.

Psychiatric Dictionary. 6th ed. New York: Oxford University Press, 1989.

Rama, S., R., Ballentine, and S. Ajaya. *Yoga and Psychotherapy: The Evolution of Consciousness.* Honesdale, PA: Himalayan International Institute of Yoga Science and Philosophy, 1981.

Randall, J. *The Career of Philosophy: From the Middle Ages to the Enlightenment.* Vol. 1. New York: Columbia University Press, 1962.

Raudsepp, E. "Can You Trust Your Hunches? Intuitive Thinking Is a Valid Decision-Making Aid." *Administrative Management* 42, no. 10 (1981): 34-54.

Ray, M. "Sharing the Wisdom: A Report of an Intuition Network Program." *Intuition at Work: Pathways to Unlimited Possibilities.* San Francisco: New Leaders Press/Sterling & Stone, Inc., 1996.

Richards, R., D. K. Kinney, M. Benet, and A. P. C. Merzel. "Assessing Everyday Creativity: Characteristics of the Lifetime Creativity Scales and Validation with Three Large Samples." *Journal of Personality and Social Psychology* 54, no. 3 (1988): 476-485.

Rico, G. *Writing the Natural Way: Using Right-Brain Techniques to Release Your Expressive Powers.* Los Angeles: J. P. Tarcher, 1983.

Rockenstein, Z. "Intuitive Processes in Executive Decision Making." *Journal of Creative Behavior* 22, no. 2 (1988): 77-84.

Rosanoff, N. *Intuition Workout: A Practical Guide to Discovering and Developing Your Inner Knowing.* Santa Rosa, CA: Aslan Publishing, 1991.

———. "Making the Workplace Safe for Intuition." *Intuition at Work: Pathways to Unlimited Possibilities.* San Francisco: New Leaders Press/Sterling & Stone, Inc., 1996.

Rothberg, D. "Theories of Inquiry: A Short Glossary." Unpublished paper, Saybrook Institute, San Francisco, 1991.

Rousseau, J. *Emile.* Translated by B. Foxley. London: J. M. Dent & Sons Ltd., 1911.

Rowan, R. *The Intuitive Manager.* Boston: Little, Brown and Company, 1986.

Salisbury, A. "Sharpening Your Sixth Sense." *Executive Update: The Magazine for Savvy Association Professionals.* Washington, DC: Greater Washington Society of Association Executives, Dec. 2002: 40–41.

———. *Determining Possible Incidents of Intuition in Participants Utilizing a Self-Hypnosis Audiotape.* Frisco, CO: Salisbury Corp., 1998.

———. *Transpersonal Hypnotherapy Institute: Professional Home Study Certification Trainings and Educational Products Catalog,* no. 16, vol. 2, Golden, CO: Transpersonal Hypnotherapy Institute, Inc., 2006.

Satprem. *Sri Aurobindo or the Adventure of Consciousness.* New York: Institute for Evolutionary Research, 1984.

Schermerhorn, J., Jr. *Management for Productivity.* New York: John Wiley & Sons, 1989.

Schopenhauer, A. *The World as Will and Representation.* Translated by E. Payne. New York: Dover, 1969.

Schwab, L. "No Static in Your Attic: Tapping into Your Creative and Intuitive Abilities." *Journal of Creative Behavior* 25, no. 3 (1991): 256-262.

Schwarz, J. *Human Energy Systems.* New York: E. P. Dutton, 1980.

———. *Voluntary Controls: Exercises for Creative Meditation and for Activating the Potential of the Chakras.* New York: E. P. Dutton, 1978.

Shealy, C. N. Interviewed by the author, August 1998.

———. *90 Days to Self-Help.* New York: Bantam Books, 1980.

———. and C. M. Myss. *The Creation of Health: Merging Traditional Medicine with Intuitive Diagnosis.* Walpole, NH: Stillpoint Publishing, 1988.

Sorokin, P. A. *The Crisis of Our Age: The Social and Cultural Outlook.* New York: E. P. Dutton & Co., 1941.

Spinoza, B. *The Collected Works of Spinoza.* Translated by E. Curley. Princeton, NJ: Princeton University Press, 1985.

Strunz, F. "Preconscious Mental Activity and Scientific Problem-Solving: A Critique of the Kekule Dream Controversy." *Dreaming* 3, no. 4 (1993): 281-294.

Sue, D. and S. Sue, *Understanding Abnormal Behavior.* 4th ed. Boston: Houghton, Mifflin Co., 1994.

Sullivan, D. "Portrait of a Prophet." *Omni* 14, no. 7 (1992): 40-50.

Taggart, W. (Faculty member, Department of Management, Florida International University.) Telephone interview with the author, March 1996.

Tellegen, A., and G. Atkinson. "Openness to Absorbing and Self-Altering Experiences ('Aabsorption'): A Trait Related to Hypnotic Susceptibility." *Journal of Abnormal Psychology* 83 (1974): 268-277.

The Holy Bible: King James Version. New York: The World Publishing Company.

The Merriam-Webster Dictionary. Springfield, MA: Merriam-Webster, Inc., 1994.

The Penguin Dictionary of Psychology. London: Penguin Group, 1985.

Trivieri, L., Jr., and The American Holistic Medical Association, *The American Holistic Medical Association's Guide to Holistic Health: Healing Therapies for Optimal Wellness.* New York: John Wiley and Sons, Inc., 2001.

Tweed, T. A. and S. Prothero, *Asian Religions in America: A Documentary History.* New York: Oxford University Press, 1999.

Vaughan, F. E. *Awakening Intuition.* New York: Doubleday, 1979.

Vogel, G. "Scientists Probe Feelings Behind Decision-Making." *Science* 275 (1997): 1269.

Waldholz, M. "Altered States – Hypnosis Goes Mainstream," *Wall Street Journal,* Oct. 7, 2003.

Wallas, G. *The Art of Thought*. London: Jonathan Cape Ltd., 1926.

Wanless, James. *Intuition at Work and at Home and at Play*. Boston: Red Wheel/Wheiser, 2002.

Weisberg, R. *Creativity: Genius and Other Myths*. New York: W. H. Freeman and Company, 1986.

Welles, P. S. "A Qualitative Study of Intuitive Processes as Constructed by Psychics, Mediums, and Therapists, with Possible Application to Family Therapy." *Dissertation Abstracts International* (1988), B50/03, AAC8914601.

Westcott, M. R. *Toward a Contemporary Psychology of Intuition: A Historical, Theoretical, and Empirical Inquiry*. New York: Holt, Rinehart and Winston, 1968.

Wild, K. W. *Intuition*. London: Cambridge University Press, 1938.

Williams, W. W. *Saint Bernard of Clairvaux*. Manchester, England: Manchester University Press, 1935.

Winkler, F. E. *Man: The Bridge Between Two Worlds*. New York: Harper & Row, 1960.

Wonder, J., and J. Blake. "Creativity East and West: Intuition vs. Logic?" *Journal of Creative Behavior* 26, no. 3 (1992): 172-185.

Webster's Third New International Dictionary of the English Language Unabridged. Springfield, MA: G. and C. Merriam Company, 1976.

World Book Encyclopedia. Chicago: World Book, Inc., 1991.

Wycoff, J. *Mindmapping*. New York: Berkley Books/Penguin Putnam, Inc., 1991.

Yogananda, P. *Autobiography of a Yogi*. Los Angeles: Self-Realization Fellowship, 1993.

———. *The Law of Success*. Los Angeles: Self-Realization Fellowship, 1990.

Zukav, G. *The Seat of the Soul*. New York: Simon & Schuster, 1990.

INDEX

ABOUT THE AUTHOR

 Anne Salisbury, Ph.D., MA, MBA, is a sought-after speaker and trainer. Her clients represent a broad base—from corporate to entrepreneurial, from associations to individuals. She provides business consulting, intuitive counseling, energy clearing/feng shui and pet psychic readings. Anne works worldwide with her many clients, either in person or by phone.

Dr. Salisbury has been involved in meditation, dreamwork, hypnotherapy and intuitive skills development since the 1970s. She holds advanced degrees in psychology and business and an undergraduate degree in art.

In 1990, she founded the Transpersonal Hypnotherapy Institute, a Board of Education approved school that has certified thousands of individuals through programs she developed. She co-founded Intuitive Advantage, Inc., a consulting firm in Golden Colorado, with her husband Greg Meyerhoff. Together they developed the *Eureka System.*^{SM}

She has served on boards and received awards from the National Association of Women Business Owners among others. Her travels have taken her around the globe, including meetings with the Dalai Lama and Mother Teresa in India.

Visit *GoIntuition.com* and *TranspersonalInstitute.com* for more information.

LEARN MORE ...

Speaking—Bring *Eureka!* and Intuition to Your Workplace or Organization

Anne Salisbury and Greg Meyerhoff are available for speeches, seminars and training on the topic of intuition including the *Eureka! System*[SM] of *ACT and LEAP.*[SM] (visit *GoIntuition.com*)

Consulting—Receive Private Information

Anne and Greg also provide business consulting, intuitive counseling, energy clearing/feng shui and pet psychic readings either in person or over the phone. (visit *GoIntuition.com*)

Distance Learning—Improve Your Intuition with Ease

Increase your ability to access intuition with comprehensive distance learning Intuitive Skills courses. Through listening to lively lectures and absorbing meditations on CDs for just a few minutes every day, you can achieve amazing results—decrease stress, increase focus, improve your decision making ability, and tap into your intuitive abilities. (visit *GoIntuition.com*)

Professional Training— Help Others Tap Into Their Intuition

Become a professional Certified Hypnotherapist through distance learning. Watch DVDs of live classes and receive personal support while enrolled. The Transpersonal Hypnotherapy Institute is approved by the Colorado Board of Education. Licensed Clinical Social Workers, Marriage and Family Therapists, Registered Nurses, and others can receive continuing education units. (visit *TranspersonalInstitute.com*)

Please visit Anne F. Salisbury, Ph.D., at
GoIntuition.com (main site)
TranspersonalInstitute.com (distance learning)

BONUS GIFTS

Go Intuition eNewsletter

You can continue to be informed. Sign up to receive your free *Go Intuition eNewsletter* that focuses on intuition. Each one embodies a nugget of truth that you can relate to immediately.

• Visit *GoIntuition.com* for your *Free eNewsletter.*

10-Minute Self-Hypnosis Audio

Get your free audio download of the self-hypnosis script, read by Anne and as seen in this book. Use this *10-Minute Self-Hypnosis Audio* as a practice tool for accessing your intuition. Play it on your computer or burn it to a CD. The more you play it, the better the results. This can make it easier for you to start communicating with your intuitive wisdom.

• Visit *GoIntuition.com* and click on Free Downloads for your Free Self-Hypnosis Audio.

COMING SOON ...

The Intuition Factor

In *Eureka! Understanding and Using the Power of Your Intuition,* you learned everything you need to know about the history and workings of intuition. You learned valuable techniques for accessing it, including meditation, self-hypnosis and dreamwork.

Soon you will be able to discover new ways to increase your intuitive abilities. *The Intuition Factor,* the upcoming book by Anne Salisbury, Ph.D., and Greg Meyerhoff, shows you how to develop a deep relationship with your intuition.

In *The Intuition Factor,* you are taken on a journey into your heart where you personally experience what it feels like to live in partnership with your intuition.

The Intuition Factor makes your journey through life a more enjoyable and successful one. It will be available early 2013. To keep updated:

- Visit *GoIntuition.com* to recieve your *Free eNewsletter* and pre-order *The Intuition Factor.*

CPSIA information can be obtained
at www.ICGtesting.com
Printed in the USA
FSOW04n1258020616
21094FS